About Access Archaeology

Access Archaeology offers a different publishing model for specialist academic material that might traditionally prove commercially unviable, perhaps due to its sheer extent or volume of colour content, or simply due to its relatively niche field of interest.

All *Access Archaeology* publications are available in open-access e-pdf format and in (on-demand) print format. The open-access model supports dissemination in areas of the world where budgets are more severely limited, and also allows individual academics from all over the world the chance to access the material privately, rather than relying solely on their university or public library. Print copies, nevertheless, remain available to individuals and institutions who need or prefer them.

The material is professionally refereed, but not peer reviewed. Copy-editing takes place prior to submission of the work for publication and is the responsibility of the author. Academics who are able to supply print-ready material are not charged any fee to publish (including making the material available in open-access). In some instances the material is type-set in-house and in these cases a small charge is passed on for layout work.

This model works for us as a publisher because we are able to publish specialist work with relatively little editorial investment. Our core effort goes into promoting the material, both in open-access and print, where *Access Archaeology* books get the same level of attention as our core peer-reviewed imprint by being included in marketing e-alerts, print catalogues, displays at academic conferences and more, supported by professional distribution worldwide.

Open-access allows for greater dissemination of the academic work than traditional print models, even lithographic printing, could ever hope to support. It is common for a new open-access e-pdf to be downloaded several hundred times in its first month since appearing on our website. Print sales of such specialist material would take years to match this figure, if indeed it ever would.

By printing 'on-demand', meanwhile, (or, as is generally the case, maintaining minimum stock quantities as small as two), we are able to ensure orders for print copies can be fulfilled without having to invest in great quantities of stock in advance. The quality of such printing has moved forward radically, even in the last few years, vastly increasing the fidelity of images (highly important in archaeology) and making colour printing more economical.

Access Archaeology is a vehicle that allows us to publish useful research, be it a PhD thesis, a catalogue of archaeological material or data, in a model that does not cost more than the income it generates.

This model may well evolve over time, but its ambition will always remain to publish archaeological material that would prove commercially unviable in traditional publishing models, without passing the expense on to the academic (author or reader).

Eastern Sudan in its Setting

The archaeology of a region far from the Nile Valley

Andrea Manzo

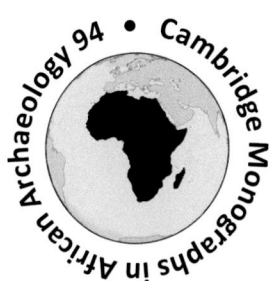

Access Archaeology

Archaeopress Publishing Ltd
Gordon House
276 Banbury Road
Oxford OX2 7ED

www.archaeopress.com

ISBN 978 1 78491 558 2
ISBN 978 1 78491 559 9 (e-Pdf)

© Archaeopress and A Manzo 2017

Cambridge Monographs in African Archaeology 94
Series Editors: Laurence Smith, Brian Stewart, Stephanie Wynne-Jones

Cover: excavation in progress in the western cemetery of the Gash Group (c. mid-3rd-early 2nd millennium BC) at site Mahal Teglinos (K 1), with in the background the Jebel Taka.

All rights reserved. No part of this book may be reproduced or transmitted,
in any form or by any means, electronic, mechanical, photocopying or otherwise,
without the prior written permission of the copyright owners.

Printed and bound in Great Britain by Marston Book Services Ltd, Oxfordshire

Contents

Preface vii

Chapter 1 Introduction 1
1.1 The archaeological exploration of the 'marginal' areas in Sudan 1
1.2 The archaeological exploration of Eastern Sudan 4
1.3 The present and past environment 7
1.4 The resources 13
1.5 Communications 14

Chapter 2 The emerging of a regional tradition (c. 6000-3000 BC) 17
2.1 The Pre-Saroba sites and the Amm Adam Group 17
2.2 The Malawiya Group 20
2.3 The Butana Group 22
2.4 A broader perspective on Mesolithic and Neolithic: the emerging complexity 28

Chapter 3 In a fledging network (c. 3000-1000 BC) 33
3.1 The Gash Group 33
3.2 The Jebel Mokram Group 43
3.3 Between Kush and Egypt 48
3.4 In the *aktionsradius* of the Pan-Grave 51

Chapter 4 The transition to nomadism (c. 1000 BC-AD 1500) 55
4.1 The Hagiz Group 55
4.2 The Khatmiya Group 58
4.3 The-Post Meroitic sites 58
4.4 Scatters of tumuli 60
4.5 The Christian sites 61
4.6 The Gergaf Group 61
4.7 The Islamic sites 64
4.8 A nomadic melting pot 65

Chapter 5 Final remarks and perspective of research 70

References 74

List of Figures

Figure 1: map of northeast Africa showing the region of Eastern Sudan (Kassala state) investigated by University of Naples 'L'Orientale' (previously Istituto Universitario Orientale) together with the Southern Methodist University (Dallas) and University of Khartoum in the Eighties, and, in 2010, by the National Corporation for Antiquities and Museums of the Sudan. 3

Figure 2: map of the region between the Gash and the Atbara rivers investigated in the Eighties by the Italian and American-Sudanese teams showing the recorded sites and the surveyed areas in the four sectors named after local toponyms. 5

Figure 3: regional cultural sequence as it was reconstructed after the investigations conducted in the Eighties compared with the cultural sequence of the Middle Nile Valley, Egypt and northern Ethiopia. 6

Figure 4: map showing the sites surveyed in the Eighties and the ones recorded by the National Corporation for Antiquities and Museums of the Sudan in 2010, also showing the complementarity of the two surveys. 8

Figure 5: satellite image of the region between the Gash and the Atbara; to be remarked the East-West oriented streams crossing the area draining towards the Atbara, the agricultural areas along the Gash, in the Gash delta and in the Shurab el-Gash sector, the eroded stripes bordering the banks of the Atbara. 9

Figure 6: the environmental variety of Eastern Sudan: a) the dry plain north of the Gash delta; b) the grassland west of the Gash delta; c) a cultivated area in the Gash delta; d) the outskirts of Kassala, in the cultivated area along the Gash river, with the Jebel Taka on the background; e) the Jebel Abu Gamal in the southern sector of the plain between the Atbara and the Gash rivers; f) the northern bank, marked by a strip of bushes, of the khor Marmadeb, a stream crossing the plain between the Atbara and the Gash rivers; g) the hills bordering the foot of the Ethio-Eritrean highlands to the east of the region. 10

Figure 7: a 2nd millennium BC grave brought to light by the heavy erosion affecting the site UA 50 when the arid conditions prevailed; to be remarked the late Mesolithic materials from the strata cut by the grave scattered among the bones. 12

Figure 8: schematic stratigraphy of site UA 53 showing the relationship between different cultural and climatic phases, as well as the environmental factors affecting the site formation processes; the soil eroded when arid conditions prevailed is highlighted by the gray colour. 12

Figure 9: map showing the occurrence of raw materials in the region and nearby as well as the main archaeological sites; aromatic resins occur in the areas highlighted in red, ebony in the brown ones, gold in the yellow ones, while white colour shows where elephants were recorded well after the mid-19th century. 14

Figure 10: fragments of Pre-Saroba ceramics: a) sherd from a knobbed ware vessel from site UA 72; b) sherd with rocker stamp packed decoration from site UA 72; c) sherd with incised wavy line decoration from site UA 42. 17

Figure 11: map showing the distribution of the Pre-Saroba sites. 18

Figure 12: late Pre-Saroba shell midden at site UA 50. 21

Figure 13: map showing the distribution of the Malawiya Group sites. 22

iii

Figure 14: fragments of Malawiya Group ceramics: a) alternated pivoted stamp decorated sherd from site UA 48; b) spaced rocker stamp decorated sherd from site UA 18; c) rim sherd of a knobbed ware bowl from site UA 18. 22

Figure 15: fragments of Butana Group ceramics: a) rim of a bowl with incised herringbone band on the lip from site UA 113; b) rim of a restricted orifice bowl with rocker impressed external decoration from site KG 23/UA 14; c) wall sherd of a bowl with herringbone incised decoration on the external surface from site KG 23/UA 14; d) rim of a black topped ware cup with parallel rows of notches on the external surface from site KG 23/UA 14; e) rim of a scraped vessel with impressions on the lip from site UA 113. 23

Figure 16: a) complete Butana Group flask from site UA 53 excavation unit VI; b) fragmentary Butana Group large conical bowl from site UA 53 excavation unit IV. 24

Figure 17: Butana Group chipped stone pick from site KG 23/UA 14. 24

Figure 18: early Butana Group shell midden in excavation unit XI at site UA 53. 26

Figure 19: map showing the distribution of the Butana Group sites. 27

Figure 20: late Butana Group grave with nine lip plugs in excavation unit XVII at site UA 53. 28

Figure 21: cawri shell associated with shell and ostrich eggshell beads from a late Butana Group grave in excavation unit XVIII at site UA 53. 28

Figure 22: fragments of Gash Group ceramics from site Mahal Teglinos (K 1): a) rim of a cup decorated with a band of punch impressions from an Early Gash Group assemblage in excavation unit XII; b) rim of a bowl with impressions on the lip from an Early Gash Group assemblage in excavation unit XII; c) rim of a cup with rail track regular rim band and light scraping outside from a Middle Gash Group assemblage in excavation unit X; d) rim of a dish with regular impressed banded decoration and black greasy slip from a Middle Gash Group assemblage in excavation unit X; e) rim of a bowl with flat lip and decorated with accurately impressed rim band from a Classic Gash Group assemblage in excavation unit VII; f) rim of a bowl with a band of wide and shallow horizontal parallel grooves from a Late Gash Group assemblage in excavation unit IX; g-h) rims of scraped ware bowls respectively with pinched and impressed decoration on the lip from Late Gash Group assemblages in excavation unit IX. 34

Figure 24: Kerma ancien I-C-Group Ib vessel found in a badly eroded double tomb in the western cemetery of site Mahal Teglinos (K 1). 35

Figure 23: sherds of Yemeni Bronze age type from Gash Group assemblages in excavation unit BSKP-Q at site Mahal Teglinos (K 1). 35

Figure 25: a Gash Group tomb in the western cemetery at site Mahal Teglinos (K 1) (excavation unit BPLF-Z/BPQA-E) characterized by a *faïence* beads bracelet and a cawri shells anklet. 36

Figure 26: rim sherds of late First Intermediate Period – early Middle Kingdom Egyptian jars and dish from a Gash Group assemblage in excavation unit X at site Mahal Teglinos (K 1). 36

Figure 27: administrative devices from site Mahal Teglinos (K 1): a) sealing from a Middle Gash Group assemblage in excavation unit X; b) mushroom shaped object, possibly a seal, from a Late Gash Group assemblage in excavation unit VI. 37

Figure 28: map showing the distribution of the Gash Group sites between the Atbara and the Gash rivers and the in the Gash delta. 38

Figure 29: detail showing the distribution of the Gash Group sites between the Atbara and the Gash rivers. 38

Figure 30: functional areas at Mahal Teglinos (K 1) in Gash Group times, the red highlight shows the settlement areas, the blue one the cemeteries, details of some structures in the different sectors are also shown. 39

Figure 31: early 2nd millennium BC mud brick structure in excavation unit BSQV-Y/BVAA-T in the central sector of the site Mahal Teglinos (K 1), plan and detail. 39

Figure 32: fragments of a large rounded tray in a fireplace of the Middle Gash Group food preparation area in excavation unit X in the central sector of the site Mahal Teglinos (K 1), and recontruction of its diameter. 40

Figure 34: Gash Group funerary stelae in the eastern cemetery of the site Mahal Teglinos (K 1). 41

Figure 33: Early Gash Group grave containing a body with contracted legs and remains of red ochre in the eastern cemetery of the site at Mahal Teglinos (K 1) (excavation unit BSPE-J/BSQA-F and BSQK).41

Figure 35: Middle Gash Group grave in the western cemetery of the site Mahal Teglinos (K 1) (excavation unit XII), it contains the main burial with the body in extended position and cawri bracelet as well as a possible sacrificed individual in highly contracted position immediately underneath the left leg of the main burial..42

Figure 36: complete vessels from the western cemetery (excavation unit XII) of the site Mahal Teglinos (K 1): a) bowl with impressed decoration from an Early Gash Group grave; b) scraped ware jar from a Middle Gash Group grave. 43

Figure 37: fragments of Jebel Mokram Group ceramics from excavation unit VI at the site Mahal Teglinos (K 1): a) rim fragment of a bowl with the upper part covered by incised net pattern; b) rim fragment of a bowl with the upper part covered by incised crossing parallel lines; c) rim fragment of a black topped bowl with the upper part covered by crossing incised parallel lines; d) fragment of a black topped vessel completely covered by rocker impressions crossed by incised lines; e) rim fragment of a bowl covered by vertical parallel grooves; f) fragment of the rim of a rim banded bowl...44

Figure 38: imported ceramic materials from Jebel Mokram Group assemblages: a) fragment of a C-Group II b vessel from excavation unit IX at site UA 53; b) fragment of an Upper Egyptian Marl A4 vessel from excavation unit IX at site UA 53..45

Figure 39: stone axe whose shape is similar to Egyptian early New Kingdom metal specimens from a Jebel Mokram Group assemblage at site UA 53. 45

Figure 40: flat oval shaped seal possibly from a Jebel Mokram Group assemblage at site JAG 1. 45

Figure 41: remains of a large circular hut or fence delimited by post holes from excavation unit IX at site UA 53..46

Figure 42: fragment of a large footed ceramic tray in situ in excavation unit VI at site Mahal Teglinos (K 1) and its reconstruction. 47

Figure 43: tomb containing a body with flexed legs and the head on a stone likely to date to Jebel Mokram Group times in excavation unit BPLF-Z/BPQA-E at site Mahal Teglinos (K 1). 48

Figure 44: map showing the distribution of the Jebel Mokram Group sites between the Atbara and the Gash rivers...48

Figure 45: map showing the distribution of the Hagiz Group sites marked by red dots, of the Post-Meroitic sites marked by blue dots, and of the Khatmiya Group sites marked by yellow dots...........55

Figure 46: remains of the stone foundations of a rounded Hagiz Group hut north of excavation unit III at site JAG 1...56

Figure 47: fragments of Hagiz Group ceramics: a) rim of a bowl with a band of oblique parallel crossing incisions from site UA 38; b) wall sherd of a vegetal tempered scraped ware vessel from site JAG 1; c) wall sherd of mat impressed ware from site UA 38; d) vegetal tempered body sherd of a vessel with vertical handle from site UA 127; e) horizontal loop handle of a vegetal tempered vessel from site UA 132. 56

Figure 48: fragments of Hagiz Group ceramics: a-b) body sherds of vessels decorated with impressed modeled ledges from site UA 129; c) side and top view of a fragment of rim of a vegetal tempered bowl with grip with incisions on it from site UA 16; d) fragment of a flaring rim cup with a groove on the lip from site UA 21. 57

Figure 49: fragments of Khatmiya Group ceramics from site K 4. 59

Figure 50: fragments of ribbed Late Antique Mediterranean amphorae from Khatmiya Group assemblages at site K 24 B. 59

Figure 51: Post-Meroitic beer-jar vessels from a site in the area of Jebel Ofreik. 59

Figure 52: Post Meroitic evidence at site JAG 1: a) the tumulus in excavation units I and II delimited by a ring of granite stones and topped by quartz pebbles; b) the funerary pit with a badly damaged skeleton at the base; c) iron arrowheads found at the base of the pit and in the niche; d) glass and stone beads found at the base of the pit and in the niche. 60

Figure 53: contracted skeleton in a tumulus in the central sector of the site at Mahal Teglinos (K 1). ...61

Figure 54: pottery decorated with incised crosses from a site in the area of Jebel Ofreik. 62

Figure 55: bench made of red bricks marking a tomb damaged by a later grave with body in extended position visible on the right in excavation unit II at site UA 126. 62

Figure 56: Gergaf Group ceramics: a) fragmentary decorated bag shaped mineral and vegetal tempered vessel, with flat rim and horizontal band of crossing incisions on the upper part of the vessel from site UA 35; b) fragmentary decorated bag shaped mineral and vegetal tempered vessel, with flat rim and horizontal band of crossing incisions on the upper part of the vessel from site UA 29. 63

Figure 57: map showing the distribution of the Gergaf Group sites marked by red dots, and of the sites with Christian materials marked by blue dots. 63

Figure 58: Gergaf Group mound with concentration of ceramic materials possibly used for funerary offerings at site UA 143. 64

Figure 59: Gergaf Group hut delimited by post holes marked by the red and white sticks in excavation unit VI of site UA 53. 65

Figure 60: a view of the Islamic cemetery with complex funerary structures at Jebel Maman. 65

Table 1: plant species identified in archaeological assemblages from Eastern Sudan. 19

Table 2: animal species identified in archaeological assemblages from Eastern Sudan. 20

Table 3: frequency of wild and domesticated mammalians in archaeological assemblages from Eastern Sudan. 25

Table 4: frequency of cattle and sheep/goat in archaeological assemblages from Eastern Sudan. 26

Preface

'We name 'archaeological cultures', 'traditions', and 'industries' with the professed intention of denoting only artifacts distributions and associations but our consciousness and these terminologies are continuously invaded by the presence of humans who produced, used, and discarded those artifacts.' (MacEachern 1998: 108)

In these words lies most of archaeological practice, and perhaps the 'invasion of humans' who are behind the objects should be regarded as natural and somehow desirable. Archaeologists certainly deal with people, although their starting point is represented by things: they reconstruct human behaviors otherwise lost forever. This is even more true when dealing with regions and peoples, who did not produce any written testimony until very recent times, as is often the case in Africa. In the case of Eastern Sudan, the region to which this book is devoted, the situation is even worst because this area -like in general the areas far from the Nile valley-, lacking both inscriptions and monumental structures, was for a longtime regarded as irrelevant or marginal in the general historical reconstruction. This book is a little token, offered to the so far silent past inhabitants of the region: I hope this will provide some preliminary insights into the contribution they gave to several crucial processes affecting the whole northeastern Africa. But the book is also dedicated to the present people of Eastern Sudan with the ambition of contributing to their awareness about the little known, but important history of the region they inhabit.

The research project in Eastern Sudan of the University 'L'Orientale' was started in 1980 by Rodolfo Fattovich. He should be thanked for his foresight. Personally, I should thank him for having introduced me to the study of the region and for allowing me to visit it in 1991 for the first time, as a student and member of the expedition he was directing. Prof. Fattovich should also be thanked for the constant encouragement, comments, and suggestions. The Expedition resumed the fieldwork after a fifteen years gap in 2010, thanks to the support of the Italian Ministry of Foreign Affairs, of the University of Naples 'L'Orientale', and of the Centro Ricerche sul Deserto Orientale. The fieldwork took place from 2012 to 2015 in the framework of the 'Futuro in Ricerca' 2012 research project code RBFR12N6WD, *Aree di transizione linguistica e culturale in Africa* (*Areas of linguistic and cultural transition in Africa*) of the Italian Ministry of Education, University and Scientific Research. I would like to express my gratitude to the granting institutions for having made this possible. I also would like to thank the Director General of the National Corporation for Antiquities and Museums of the Sudanese Government and all the Sudanese colleagues of the Corporation, as well as the Ministry of Culture, Media and Tourism of the Kassala State for their constant support and warm hospitality. In these years, the Italian Embassy in Sudan and its staff have greatly contributed to the success of the fieldwork.

This book is largely based on the fieldwork of the Italian Archaeological Expedition to the Eastern Sudan I have been directing since 2010. In addition to the important contributions made by the staff of the Expedition -some of them once students and now young colleagues-, I would like to mention that since 2014, in the framework of the Expedition, a field school made up of Sudanese and Italian students has been initiated. This book is also dedicated to these students, as a token for their passion and active participation. I would also like to remember the crucial role played by our representative and colleague from the National Corporation, Habab Idriss Ahmed.

Fieldwork is not only an exciting experience, but also prolonged absence from home. And at home too, research is often if not always a full-time job. For this reason, I would like to dedicate this work to my family and especially to Lia and Matteo for their support and patience.

Chapter 1

Introduction

1.1 The archaeological exploration of the 'marginal' areas in Sudan

A recent overview of the state of our knowledge of the Mesolithic and Neolithic phases in central Sudan complains about the fact that it is not viable to outline a settlement pattern without taking into consideration a larger area exceeding 5km to the east or to the west of the Nile (Usai 2014: 36). This very reasonable consideration can also be extended to a larger spatial scale and to the regions far away from the Nile valley such as the Western and the Eastern Desert, and Eastern Sudan as well, which is the region to which this study is devoted, and transposed to a more general level: it should be considered not viable to study the Nile valley without taking into consideration the regions east and west of it. The above referred remark is in general highly indicative of the scarce attention paid by the Nubian-Sudanese archaeology -but to some extent we may also extend it to the Egyptian archaeology- to the regions a long way from the Nile river. Even though some research projects have been launched in the deserts and marginal areas in recent years, the situation remains substantially the same today and can be certainly said that in Sudan archaeological research almost exclusively focuses on the sites and regions of the Nile valley.

This is also certainly due to environmental difficulties preventing systematic and intensive explorations of areas out of reach from the main modern centers located in the valley (Vercoutter 1994: 63-64) and consistently increasing the costs of research projects willing to focus on the regions east and west of the Nile valley as compared to research conducted near the Nile. Moreover, another factor that discourages research in the regions far from the Nile is the fact that most monumental sites are concentrated in the valley, and up to very recent times the main concern of archaeologists working in Egypt and Sudan was mainly represented by the recovery of objects relevant from an artistic point of view and of inscriptions (Welsby 2004: 12). Particularly in Sudan, archaeological research was often directly related to the construction of dams on the Nile, aimed at the production of electricity and at the improvement of the agricultural exploitation of specific areas (Mohammed Ahmed 1997: 2-3; Trigger 1994: 335-337; Welsby 2004: 14). Rescue archaeology on one hand certainly helped to extend intensive investigation to largely unexplored regions of the valley less rich in terms of monumental sites, but it also prevented the extension of the exploration of the deserts by concentrating the efforts of scholars in intensive, time-limited operations along specific traits of the Nile.

Apart from the above described factors, it should be remarked that more general cultural prejudices may have sometimes unconsciously limited research activities in places far from the Nile valley. Western scholars for many years were conditioned by the idea that civilization is an offspring of agriculture and urbanism and for this reason nothing relevant could be expected from areas today and most likely in the past mostly inhabited by nomadic livestock breeders. Interestingly, the prejudice for people living in the areas far from the river was also induced by the ancient texts -and archaeology in the Nile valley was always closely related to philology and epigraphy- depicting the inhabitants of the deserts as barbaric and uncivilized. Of course, those descriptions were the results of the highly ideological point of view of the states of the valley and of their rulers, i.e. the main producers of the texts, who always proposed themselves as guarantors of social, natural and cosmic order against the chaotic forces, often embodied in the other, in the peoples living outside of the state, i.e. outside of the valley (Barnard 2012: 6; Friedman 2002: xiii; Kuper 2002: 1, 9). Nevertheless, apart from the ideological world often depicted in the written texts, the inhabitants of the valley were always fully aware of the relevance of the relations with the desert regions and their inhabitants. This sometimes emerges from the written texts themselves: several years ago, in a study devoted to the adaptive systems in northeastern Africa in the 1st millennium BC-1st millennium AD, I remarked that in Hellenistic and Roman sources regarding the regions south of Egypt, an overwhelming part is dedicated to the regions far away from the Nile valley, mainly because several resources crucial in ancient times were concentrated there, and because the routes crossing these lands were regarded as strategic for ancient trade (Manzo 1996: 81-82, Table 3).

Leaving the Hellenistic and Roman sources apart, the awareness of the relevance of the peripheral desert areas for a full understanding of the complexity of the history of northeastern Africa is slowly emerging even among scholars. In general, this first happened in the field of prehistory, because these studies are perhaps less conditioned by research on monuments and, of course, have nothing to do with texts. Moreover, among prehistorians there is also the awareness that before the environmental changes that led to the present situation, the marginal areas could have been densely inhabited. For these reasons, the desert areas are regarded as crucial for understanding the prehistory of the valley itself. This is clearly shown by the contribution of the desert areas not only in ideas and know-how to the cultural developments in the valley itself, but also demographically to its peopling, when the environmental conditions in the deserts became drier and drier, and their inhabitants moved closer to the river (see Barnard 2012: 4; Friedman 2002). In recent years it was also demonstrated that this contribution of the deserts to the cultures of the valley may have extended to relevant ideological aspects like e.g. the cattle-cult and perhaps some astral connotations of the religions of the inhabitants of the Nile valley (see Kuper 2002: 10; Wendorf and Schild 2002: 18-19). In the meantime, scholars focusing on later phases too started realizing the potential, in terms of knowledge of the past of the whole region, of the marginal areas, and projects on the exploration of specific sectors or of specific phases, from the Bronze Age to the Late Antique period, started both in Egypt and the Sudan. In particular, the fact that the deserts and the marginal areas are increasingly regarded as an unavoidable factor in the reconstruction of the history of northeastern Africa (see Trigger 1994: 336-337) was explicitly acknowledged with the publications of collections of papers devoted to this subject (see e.g. Friedman ed. 2002; Barnard and Duistermaat eds. 2012).

Nevertheless, there is still much to be done in terms of fieldwork, particularly in Sudan. So far, only a handful of projects were specifically devoted to the exploration of the deserts and the other areas far away from the Nile there. In other cases, some sites on the fringes of the deserts were only sporadically visited and sometimes studied in the framework of projects firmly rooted in the valley (Mohammed Ahmed 1997: 5). In this perspective, the German project of the University of Cologne organized and for many years led by Rudolf Kuper, focusing on the Western Desert, in a broad area between the Wadi Howar and the Egyptian-Sudanese border, and on sites dating from prehistoric to Napatan times should be certainly mentioned (Kuper 2002: 2). On the other side of the Nile valley, the activities in the Eastern Desert were even more limited if possible, with an unsystematic survey conducted by the Centro Ricerche sul Deserto Orientale (CeRDO) of Angelo and Alfredo Castiglioni for many years (Sadr, Castiglioni and Castiglioni 1995), and the survey of the gold mines in that area conducted in the framework of a larger project also extending to the Egyptian Eastern Desert by Rosemarie and Dietrich Klemm (Klemm and Klemm 2013). It is only in recent years that an expedition of the Sudan Archaeological Research Society is revisiting some of the sites already recorded by the Castiglioni brothers in the perspective of the final publication of the data they collected (Davies 2014), a project in which I am participating (see also Manzo 2012: 79-82), and a project coordinated by the University of Khartoum started on the Red Sea coast that will certainly impact our knowledge of the Eastern Desert and Eastern Sudan.

In the same years of the German project in the Western Desert, two other projects as well, one Italian and the other American-Sudanese, started in Eastern Sudan, roughly corresponding to the present Kassala state, a region immediately east of the Atbara and delimited to the east by the southern fringes of the Red Sea hills, to the north by the Eastern Desert and to the south and southeast by the slopes of the

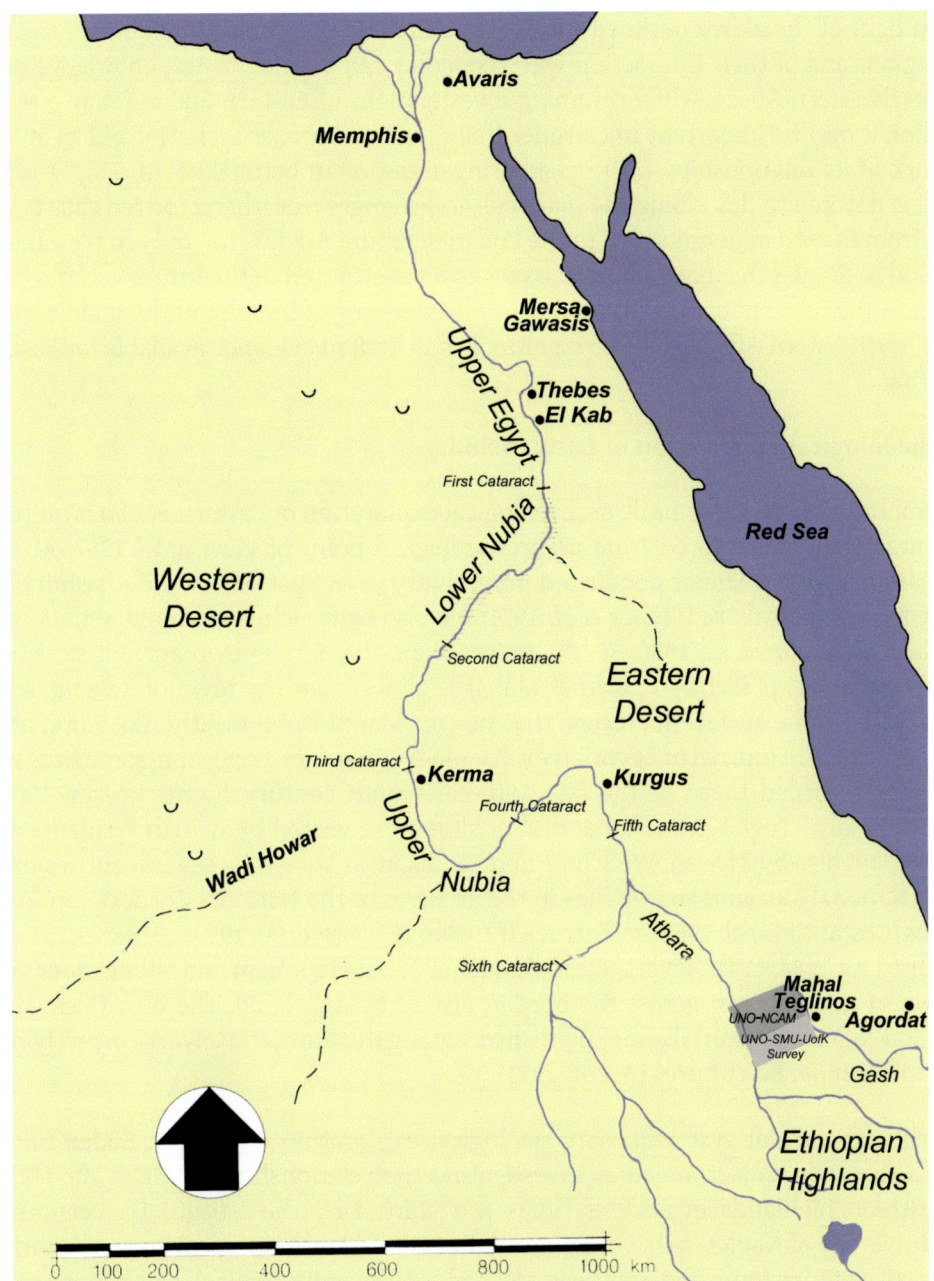

FIGURE 1: MAP OF NORTHEAST AFRICA SHOWING THE REGION OF EASTERN SUDAN (KASSALA STATE) INVESTIGATED BY UNIVERSITY OF NAPLES 'L'ORIENTALE' (PREVIOUSLY ISTITUTO UNIVERSITARIO ORIENTALE) TOGETHER WITH THE SOUTHERN METHODIST UNIVERSITY (DALLAS) AND UNIVERSITY OF KHARTOUM IN THE EIGHTIES, AND, IN 2010, BY THE NATIONAL CORPORATION FOR ANTIQUITIES AND MUSEUMS OF THE SUDAN.

Ethio-Eritrean highlands (Figure 1). A more detailed description of the exploration of the region -whose archaeology is the subject of this book - will follow. For the moment it is enough to remark that, at least in the case of the Italian project, the specific interest for an intermediate region between two centers of civilization characterized by very distinct cultural traditions like the Nile valley and the Ethio-Eritrean highlands, was well fitting in a more general interest typical of Italian archaeology in Asia and Africa after the Second World War, precisely focusing on apparently marginal areas. This distinctive interest led to important contributions to our knowledge of the ancient world like the discoveries of Ebla in Syria and Shar-i Sokhta in Afghanistan.

Therefore, in light of the above outlined issues related to the potential contributions the study of the 'marginal' regions and of their interaction with the valley can provide to the knowledge of the past of the whole northeastern Africa, while resuming investigations of Eastern Sudan (Manzo *et al.* 2011: 1-2, 2012: 1), I think it may be important to consider that area in a broader scenario, and to investigate it in the framework of its relationships with neighboring areas, often better known. This study, motivated by this need, is devoted to describing the main cultural changes that characterized the region in a very long period, from the 6th millennium BC to the 2nd millennium AD. It is not only to try a first attempt at a synthesis and to discuss the many debated issues to be confronted in the future with further research, but also to show the relevant contribution to our understanding of the past of the middle Nile valley and of the whole northeastern Africa, that the admittedly still limited evidence available for Eastern Sudan is already offering.

1.2 The archaeological exploration of Eastern Sudan

As already emphasized, the systematic archaeological exploration of Eastern Sudan is quite recent. The region was practically unexplored from an archaeological point of view until 1967. At that time an American team led by Joel Shiner conducted preliminary investigations in the Khashm el-Girba area, immediately East of the Atbara (Shiner *et al.* 1971; see also Fattovich, Marks and Mohammed Ali 1984: 176; Marks and Mohammed Ali 1980: 32-33). Before then, the only known ancient sites in the region were 'Mahal Daqlianus', presently known as Mahal Teglinos, near the town of Kassala, where in 1917 Crowfoot collected some surface materials that he considered to be mostly Aksumite, and which he published in an article in Journal of Egyptian Archaeology (Crowfoot 1928), and some sites with possible Islamic remains recorded there in the late 19th-early 20th century (Conti Rossini 1903; Crowfoot 1922). Later on, Mahal Teglinos and a handful of sites were visited by British residents and amateur archaeologists, but also by Kirwan, Wellcome and Sandison, as shown by several entries in the register of the Sudan National Museum and by files in the archives of the National Corporation for Antiquities and Museums (Costantini *et al.* 1982: 31; Fattovich 1989b: 223, 1989e: 90, 1993a: 228-229; Fattovich, Marks and Mohammed Ali 1984: 174). Nevertheless, Dandaneit, Shabeit, Kokan and Ntanei, four sites near the Eritrean town of Agordat, just across the border, visited by Arkell, are the only ones whose general description and collected materials were published: among the finds, some were correctly related to the Nubian 2nd millennium BC cultures (Arkell 1954).

The first large program of systematic archaeological exploration of Eastern Sudan only started in 1980, when a research project aimed at investigating the relationships between the Nile valley and the Ethio-Eritrean highlands in ancient times was started by the Istituto Universitario Orientale -presently University of Naples 'L'Orientale'-, and the Butana Archaeological Project, jointly sponsored by the University of Khartoum and Southern Methodist University (Dallas), was begun with the aim of studying the relationships between Eastern Sudan and the Nile valley in the 'Neolithic' phase, without overlooking other possible links to more southern regions in prehistoric times (Fattovich, Marks and Mohammed Ali 1984: 173-174; see also Fattovich 1982, 1989e: 91-93, Marks and Fattovich 1989: 451; Marks and Mohammed Ali 1980: 34-35). The two teams were conducting a systematic extensive survey of the area (Sadr 1990: 66-67) in the framework of a close collaboration established since the very beginning of their activities (Marks and Fattovich 1989: 451) (Figure 2). They were able to considerably increase the number of the known sites, and this part of the collaborative work resulted in one of the very few examples of territorial studies in the Nubian-Sudanese archaeology (Sadr 1988, 1991), together with the earlier study of the Lower Nubian settlement pattern (Trigger 1965), the investigation of the settlement pattern in the Wadi Howar (Keding 2004), and, in more recent times, similar studies conducted in specific areas of Upper Nubia (Welsby ed. 2001), in the region of the Third Cataract (Edwards, Osman *et al.* 2011) and for Meroitic Upper Nubia (Edwards 1989). The 256 sites surveyed in Eastern Sudan were labeled according to the sector where they were located, in turn named after local toponyms (Sadr

1988: 389-390, Fig. 7, 1991: 36-37) (see again Figure 2). The name of each site resulted from the capital abbreviation of the name of the sector followed by the progressive number of the sites recorded in the sector itself. Excavations, in most cases limited test pits, were conducted at 17 sites, both with the aim of evaluating the depth of the stratified deposit as well as in order to establish the relative chronology among the cultural units which were defined (Marks and Fattovich 1989: 453; Sadr 1988: 391, 1991: 37-38). In particular, the Italian expedition contributed to the reconstruction of the history of the region, especially through a more extensive excavation of some sectors of the site of Mahal Teglinos, since then labeled according to the name of the sector where it was located as Kassala (abbreviation K) 1 (Fattovich 1989b, 1991a, 1993a).

This research activity resulted in the establishment of a long regional cultural sequence starting in the 6th millennium BC and ending in the 2nd millennium AD (Fattovich, Marks and Mohammed Ali 1984; Fattovich 1989a: 481, 1989b: 226-227, 1991a: 117-118, 1990a: 11, 1993a: 226-227; Fattovich, Sadr and Vitagliano 1988-1989: 333-335; Marks and Fattovich 1989) (Figure 3). Its main phases, conventionally

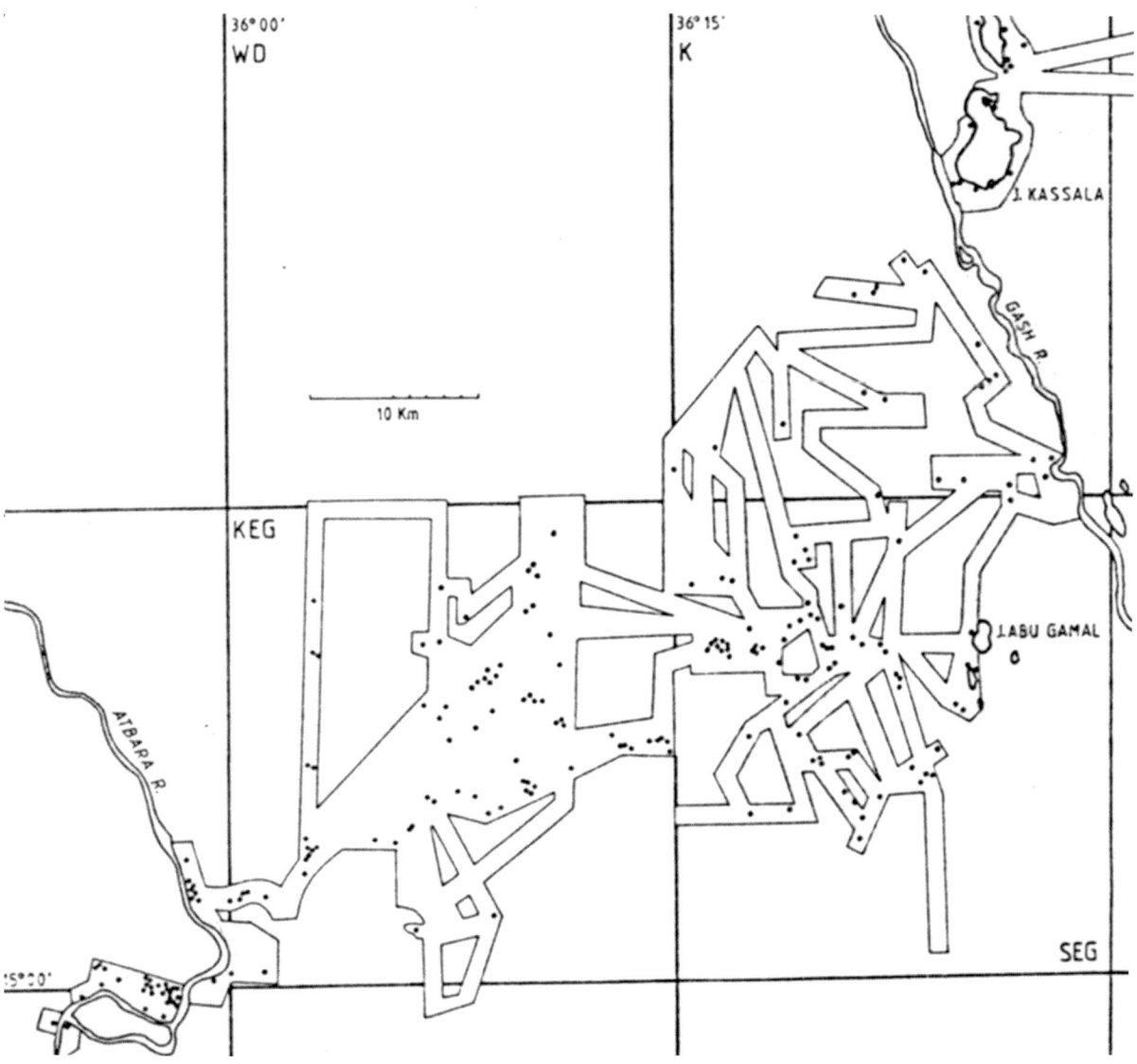

FIGURE 2: MAP OF THE REGION BETWEEN THE GASH AND THE ATBARA RIVERS INVESTIGATED IN THE EIGHTIES BY THE ITALIAN AND AMERICAN-SUDANESE TEAMS SHOWING THE RECORDED SITES AND THE SURVEYED AREAS IN THE FOUR SECTORS NAMED AFTER LOCAL TOPONYMS (FROM SADR 1991).

labeled with names of places in the region are as follows:

- Pre-Saroba Phase roughly dating to the 6th millennium BC and represented by some sites between the Gash and the Atbara rivers and by the sites of the Amm Adam Group in the Gash delta;

- Saroba Phase roughly dating to the 5th millennium BC and represented by the sites of the Malawiya Group located between the Gash and the Atbara rivers;

- Kassala Phase dating to the 4th-early 1st millennia BC and represented by three successive groups of sites labeled as Butana Group, Gash Group and Jebel Mokram Group all occurring between the Atbara and the Gash rivers, and, in the case of the Gash Group, also extending to the Gash delta;

- Taka Phase dating to the early 1st millennium BC-late 1st millennium AD and represented by the sites of the Hagiz Group between the Gash and the Atbara rivers and by a handful of Khatmiya Group sites east of Kassala, where there are also some tumuli likely dating to this phase, as well as a couple of Post-Meroitic sites near Jebel Ofreik and in the region between the Gash and the Atbara, and by a few Christian sites north of Kassala.

The Taka Phase is followed by the Gergaf Group, whose sites occur between the Gash and the Atbara rivers and which is dated around the mid-2nd millennium AD.

The features characterizing each phase, as well as the main issues in terms of results of the research as well as of ongoing scientific debate and perspective of research will be discussed more systematically and with more details in the following chapters.

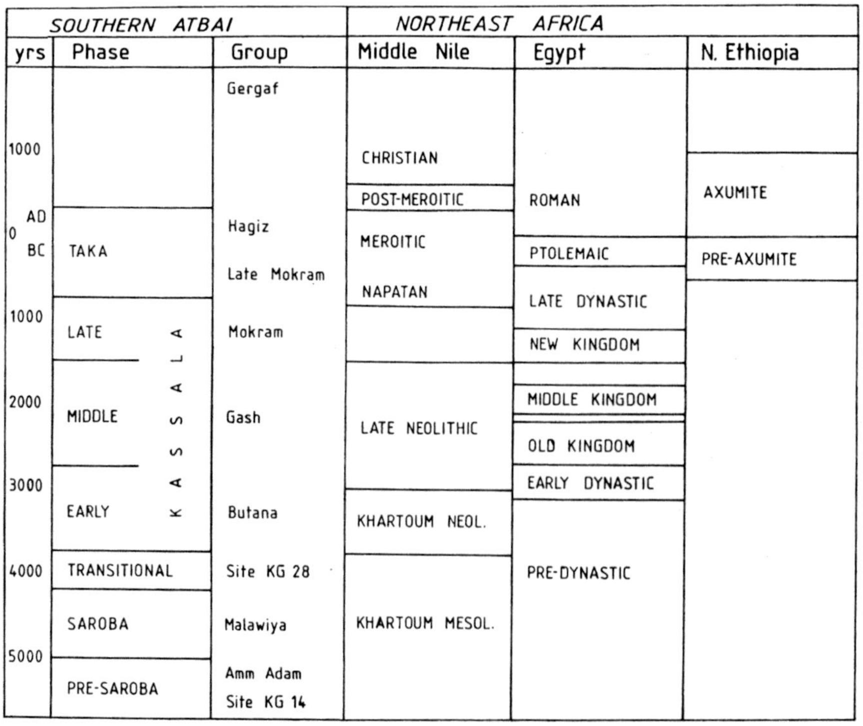

	SOUTHERN ATBAI		NORTHEAST AFRICA		
yrs	Phase	Group	Middle Nile	Egypt	N. Ethiopia
		Gergaf			
1000			CHRISTIAN		
			POST-MEROITIC	ROMAN	AXUMITE
AD 0 BC	TAKA	Hagiz	MEROITIC	PTOLEMAIC	PRE-AXUMITE
		Late Mokram	NAPATAN	LATE DYNASTIC	
1000	LATE	Mokram		NEW KINGDOM	
		K			
2000	MIDDLE	A S S Gash	LATE NEOLITHIC	MIDDLE KINGDOM	
		A		OLD KINGDOM	
3000	EARLY	L A Butana	KHARTOUM NEOL.	EARLY DYNASTIC	
4000	TRANSITIONAL	Site KG 28		PRE-DYNASTIC	
	SAROBA	Malawiya	KHARTOUM MESOL.		
5000	PRE-SAROBA	Amm Adam Site KG 14			

FIGURE 3: REGIONAL CULTURAL SEQUENCE AS IT WAS RECONSTRUCTED AFTER THE INVESTIGATIONS CONDUCTED IN THE EIGHTIES COMPARED WITH THE CULTURAL SEQUENCE OF THE MIDDLE NILE VALLEY, EGYPT AND NORTHERN ETHIOPIA (MODIFIED FROM SADR 1991).

In addition to outlining the general cultural sequence of Eastern Atbai, some major turning points in the history of the region too, were already identified in the 1980s (Fattovich 1991a: 128-129, 1990a: 30-31, 1993b: 443-444; Fattovich, Sadr and Vitagliano 1988-1989: 348-352; Marks and Sadr 1988; Sadr 1987, 1988, 1990): the process of adopting domestic livestock in the region, and of cultivating plants took place at least from the 4th millennium BC, while the progressive shift to a nomadic and pastoral style of life started in the mid-2nd millennium BC; the rise of hierarchic societies in the region as well as the progressive inclusion of the region in a broad network of relations extending from Egypt to the Yemeni highlands characterizing the 3rd and 2nd millennia BC were outlined. Moreover, a regional ceramic tradition, labeled Atbai Ceramic Tradition and characterized, from its origins in the 5th millennium BC up to its end in the late 1st millennium AD, by the occurrence of scraped ware -a distinctive treatment of the surfaces of the vessels which were combed both on the inside and outside- was defined (Fattovich, Marks and Mohammed Ali 1984: 176-178; Fattovich 1990a: 10-11; Marks and Fattovich 1989: 453; Marks and Sadr 1988: 71).

In 2010 the Italian Archaeological Expedition to the Eastern Sudan of the University of Naples 'L'Orientale' resumed the fieldwork after a gap of fifteen years (see Manzo *et al.* 2011: 1-2, 2012: 1) in order to get a better knowledge of the relationships between Eastern Sudan and Upper Nubia, to investigate the possible relationships between the cultures of Eastern Sudan, the Red Sea coast and the Eastern Desert, to increase our knowledge of some phases in the cultural sequence of the area which were only marginally investigated, to elaborate a broader palaeoenvironmental model for the whole region to be related with archaeological remains by means of systematic geo-archaeological studies, as well as to continue the archaeozoological and palaeobotanical studies aimed at getting a better definition of the ancient economy and man-environment relationships in the region.

In addition to those tasks, the Italian Archaeological Expedition to the Eastern Sudan had to face a further and more urgent challenge related to rescue archaeology. Actually, when the decision of resuming the fieldwork was taken in 2010, it become clear that the cultural heritage of the region under investigation was going to be heavily affected by the ongoing construction of new dams on the Atbara and Setit rivers and by an irrigated agricultural scheme in the whole area between the Gash and the Atbara (Upper Atbara Agricultural Irrigated Scheme). Already, before the fieldwork of the Italian expedition was resumed, in June 2010 the National Corporation for Antiquities and Museums of the Sudan surveyed the endangered area and recorded 136 sites which were labeled with the abbreviation UA (Upper Atbara) followed by a progressive number. To this number, starting from 2011, other twenty-one sites were added by the Italian expedition (see Manzo *et. al.* 2012: 123; Manzo 2015: 234). It should be stressed that these salvage archaeological activities are also contributing to the overall archaeological research in the region, as the area affected by the irrigation scheme and surveyed in 2010 by the National Corporation for Antiquities and Museums largely complements the one surveyed in the 1980s by the Italian and American-Sudanese teams (Manzo *et al.* 2012: 1) (Figure 4).

Since 2010 the Italian Archaeological Expedition to the Eastern Sudan has conducted six field seasons and started investigations in new sectors of the site of Mahal Teglinos (K1), at the site of Jebel Abu Gamal (JAG) 1, as well as at several sites endangered by the irrigation scheme such as UA14 (previously labeled as KG23), UA53, UA50, UA126, UA129, and UA143 (Manzo *et al.* 2011, 2012; Manzo 2013, 2014a, 2015, 2016).

1.3 The present and past environment

Eastern Sudan is the region also labeled as southern Atbai located east of the Atbara river, the last big tributary of the Nile. It is bordered to the south and south-east by the Eritrean-Ethiopian highlands, to the north and north-east by the southern fringes of the Eastern Desert and the Red Sea hills (Barbour 1961: 219, 222) (Figure 5). The region is almost completely flat (see e.g. Figure 6, a-c, f) except for a few granite hill masses, such as the Jebel Taka (Figure 6 d), near Kassala and Jebel Abu Gamal south-west of it (Figure 6 e), and it is traditionally inhabited mainly by groups of livestock breeders who periodically

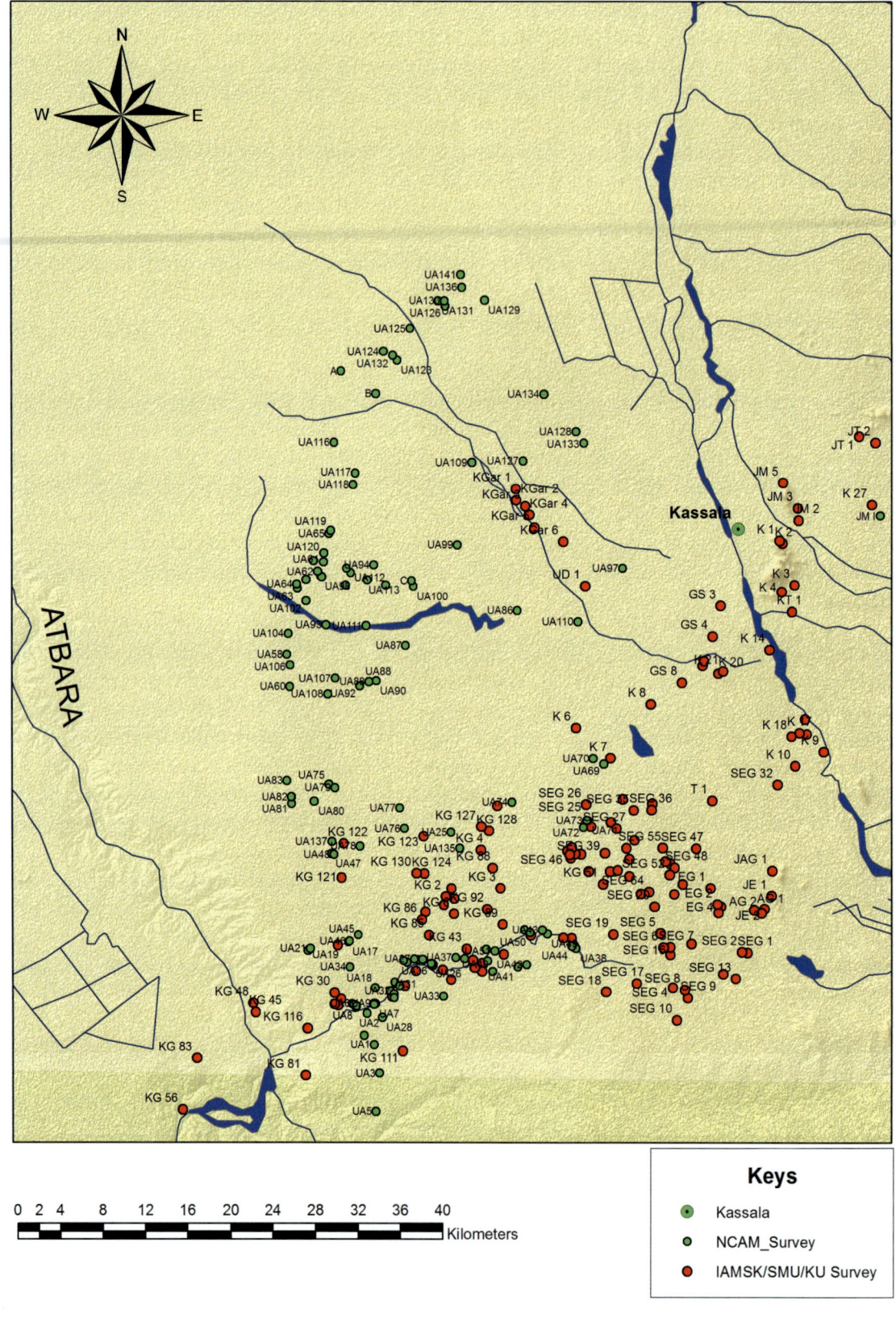

Figure 4: map showing the sites surveyed in the Eighties and the ones recorded by the National Corporation for Antiquities and Museums of the Sudan in 2010, also showing the complementarity of the two surveys (elaborated by V. Zoppi).

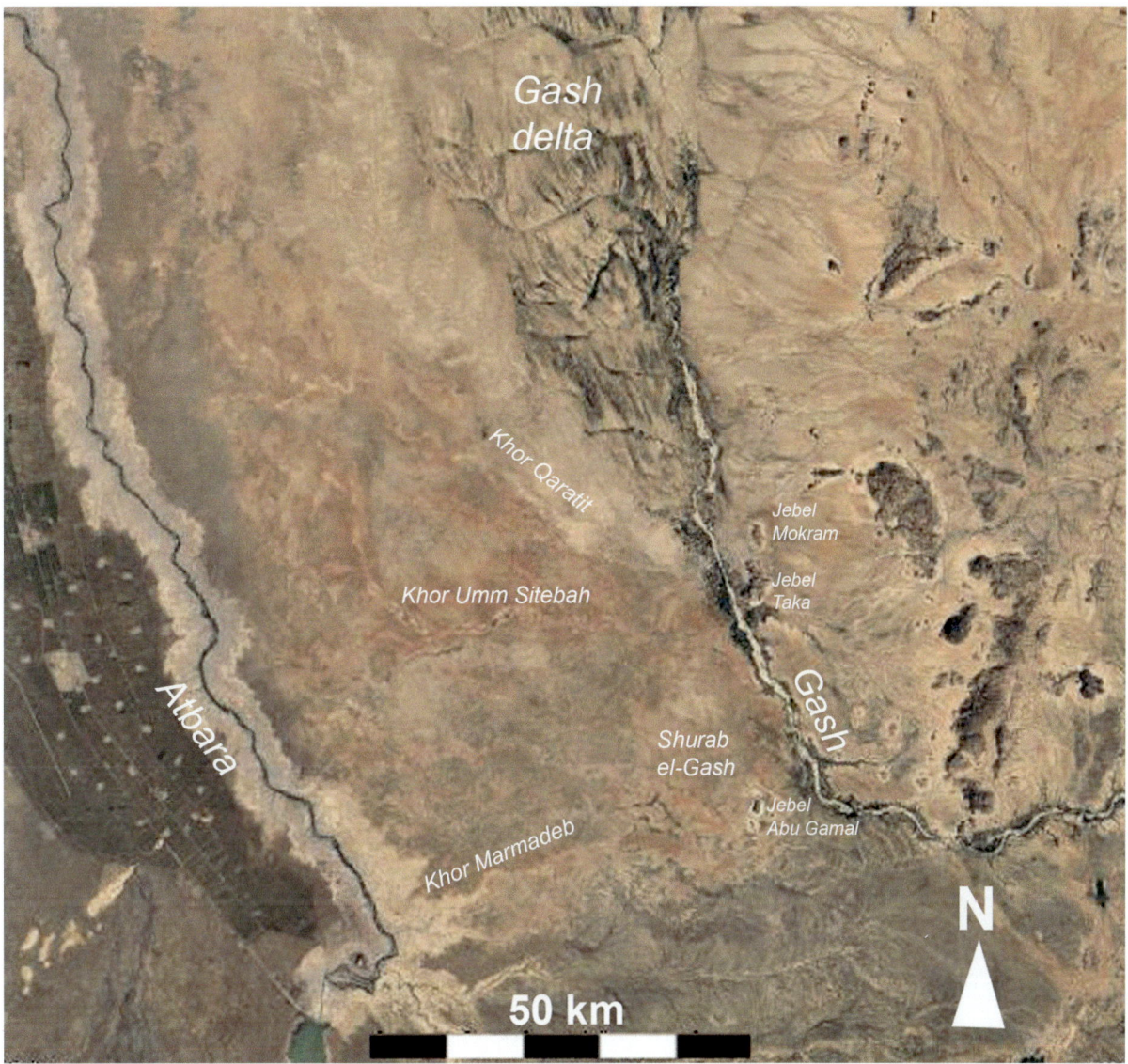

Figure 5: satellite image of the region between the Gash and the Atbara; to be remarked the East-West oriented streams crossing the area draining towards the Atbara, the agricultural areas along the Gash, in the Gash delta and in the Shurab el-Gash sector, the eroded stripes bordering the banks of the Atbara (modified Google Earth image).

move across it, following the availability of resources determined by the monsoon rains affecting the area in the summer, in a generally arid climate, and by the seasonal water made available by the two rivers crossing the region and draining from the Ethio-Eritrean highlands, i.e. the Atbara and the Gash (Barbour 1961: 26-29, 38-39, 219, 225-226; Sadr 1991: 25-26; Shiner *et al.* 1971: 294). Interestingly too is the fact that the rains are not homogeneously distributed, but more abundant in places closer to the slopes of the Ethio-Eritrean highlands i.e. in the southeastern parts of the region (Barbour 1961: 38-39, Fig. 21, 22) (Figure 6 g). The areas along the banks of the Gash, and in the Gash delta as well as some specific spots between the Gash and the Atbara rivers, like the Shurab el-Gash area, are richer in water and soil resources and are therefore more suitable for agricultural exploitation (Figure 6 c-d), while the rest of the region offers more or less rich grazing (Barbour 1961: 37, 128, 219; Cumming 1937: 1-2; Sadr 1991: 27-29; Worrall 1960: 108-109) (Figure 6 b). The flora of the region is mainly characterized by annual grasses, bushes and acacia trees (Wickens 1982). The economic potential of the area between Gash and Atbara is also enhanced by the

six major streams with an east-west orientation crossing it and flowing towards the basin of the Atbara due to the terrain's gentle inclination down from the east, where the Red Sea hills and the footslopes of the Ethio-Eritrean plateau are located, to the west (Shiner *et al.* 1971: 296) (Figure 6 f). On the contrary, the banks of the Atbara were affected by severe erosion that brought to light older terraces very poor in terms of productive land (Shiner *et al.* 1971: 293-294).

These general conditions determining the distribution of resources such as fertile land and grazing areas clearly affect the life style and economic activities of the present inhabitants of the region (Barbour 1961: 221-226; Cumming 1937: 2-3; Sadr 1991: 26-30). They belong to several different groups, mainly represented by the Hadendowa, Halenga and Beni Amer. All are part of the broader Beja family, and traditionally nomadic herdsmen. Then, the Rashaida, who arrived recently from Arabia and are basically devoted to camel breeding, and the Nubians, farmers, traders and administrators, mainly concentrating in the towns and in the areas more suitable for agriculture. Numerically smaller groups are represented by the Barya (Nara) and the Kunama, farmers and livestock breeders: they were regarded as a very recent presence in the region as several of them moved in from Eritrea in the last decades, but these groups may have been present in Eastern Sudan in ancient times too (Fattovich 1994: 36-42). From the linguistic point of view, these people speak Semitic (Arabic), Cushitic (Beja) and Nilo-Saharan (Nara and Kunama) languages (Thompson 1976: 598-600).

FIGURE 6: THE ENVIRONMENTAL VARIETY OF EASTERN SUDAN: A) THE DRY PLAIN NORTH OF THE GASH DELTA; B) THE GRASSLAND WEST OF THE GASH DELTA; C) A CULTIVATED AREA IN THE GASH DELTA; D) THE OUTSKIRTS OF KASSALA, IN THE CULTIVATED AREA ALONG THE GASH RIVER, WITH THE JEBEL TAKA ON THE BACKGROUND; E) THE JEBEL ABU GAMAL IN THE SOUTHERN SECTOR OF THE PLAIN BETWEEN THE ATBARA AND THE GASH RIVERS; F) THE NORTHERN BANK, MARKED BY A STRIP OF BUSHES, OF THE KHOR MARMADEB, A STREAM CROSSING THE PLAIN BETWEEN THE ATBARA AND THE GASH RIVERS; G) THE HILLS BORDERING THE FOOT OF THE ETHIO-ERITREAN HIGHLANDS TO THE EAST OF THE REGION.

The environmental conditions of the region certainly underwent several changes through the period dealt with in this book. In general, the region was involved in the climatic trends affecting the whole northeastern Africa, with wetter conditions in the earliest part of the Holocene, later some drier oscillations around the mid-Holocene -a relevant one perhaps started at the beginning of the 6th millennium BC-, and more arid conditions set by the mid-3rd millennium BC ca., although sensible differences were remarked from north to south in the moment when the change of the trend towards drier condition became evident (Bubenzer et al. 2007; Kuper and Kröpelin 2006; Nicoll 2001, 2004 see also Williams et al. 2015: 85-87; Lesur et al. 2013: 149). In Eastern Sudan, this presumably entailed the southward and eastward shift of the deciduous savanna woodland as it was previously proposed (Wickens 1975: 52; see also Sadr 1991: 30, Fig. 3.6). Nevertheless, it is likely that this was a progressively slow and not coherent process, and it seems very possible that our region, like central Sudan, was only affected by the general climatic trend very gradually, and likely not from its very beginning (Williams 2009; Williams et al. 2010).

The palaeoenvironmental studies undertaken after 2010 are presently in progress and will certainly enrich our reconstruction, adding insights into the complexity that characterized the process. Nevertheless, the above outlined general trend also seems to be confirmed by few geoarchaeological observations conducted recently in some of the sites under investigation in Eastern Sudan such as Mahal Teglinos (K 1), UA 53 and UA 50. In particular, at UA 50, in a site located in the flat area between the Gash and the Atbara whose investigation is still in progress, clay strata originating from the activity of a stream near the site covered a living surface dated to ca. 5000 BC where traces of exploitation of land snails, clearly compatible with humid environment, were recorded (see Manzo 2016: 194). The fact that some of the materials dating back to that phase, had moved and embedded in later clay strata may even suggest that the site was periodically flooded after 5000 BC. Later on graves, possibly dating back to the 2nd millennium BC, were excavated in these strata, but an intense erosive phase suggesting reduced wadi activity and prevailing wind erosion led to the destruction of the upper part of their pits, also bringing to light the 5000 BC living floor (Figure 7). At UA 53, the formation of thick clay strata possibly related to the intense activity of a nearby stream continued after the early 4th millennium BC, while an impressive erosion suggesting a reduced activity of the stream, in turn related to the decrease of the rains, seems to have already affected the site in the 2nd millennium BC and led to the almost complete erosion of the clay strata covering an early 4th millennium BC living surface as well as of the upper pits of the late 4th millennium BC graves excavated in these clay strata (Manzo et al. 2012: 9, 106; Manzo 2014a: 386) (Figure 8). At Mahal Teglinos (K 1), a small lake in the western sector of the site progressively dried up to a complete disappearance around 2000 BC (Manzo 2014a: 386, 2015: 235).

Interestingly, both the evidence from UA 50 and UA 53 may suggests that the drier oscillations around the mid-Holocene well known in the Nile valley may not have been so relevant in our region, and that more humid conditions may have locally continued longer. Actually, drier conditions may have been evident from the 3rd millennium BC onwards, but their effects were again gradual, as suggested by the drying of the small lake at Mahal Teglinos (K 1) only in the early 2nd millennium BC. Nevertheless, already in the 2nd millennium BC intense erosive processes suggesting drier climatic conditions had taken place at UA 53. This specific palaeoenvironmental trend may perhaps not be related only to the latitude of our region, but also to the geographic closeness between Eastern Sudan and the Ethio-Eritrean highlands: this may have somehow mitigated the effects of the general trend towards increasing aridity in the region, with the connected later disappearance of internal basins and lakes, as compared to regions to the west and to the north. Moreover, the presence of the foothills of the Red Sea hills and of the Ethio-Eritrean highlands up to date still justifies the occurrence of more intense rains in the eastern sector of the region (see above), and this pattern may have also been so in ancient times, and may have determined the continuation of local wetter condition in that sector.

Figure 7: a 2nd millennium BC grave brought to light by the heavy erosion affecting the site UA 50 when the arid conditions prevailed; to be remarked the late Mesolithic materials from the strata cut by the grave scattered among the bones.

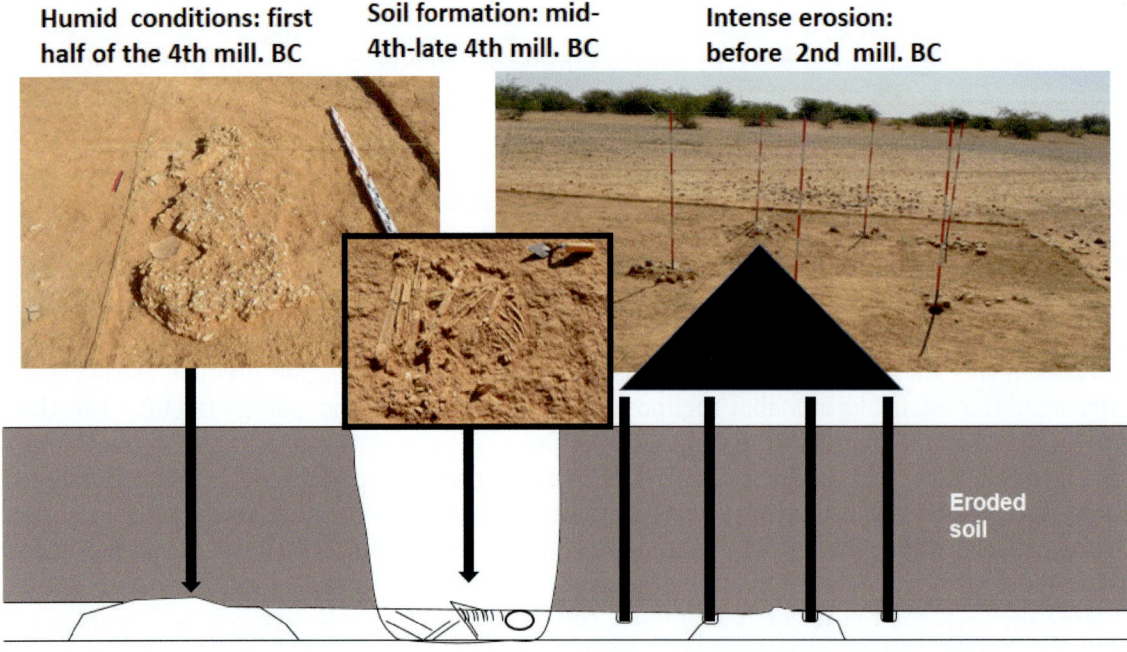

Figure 8: schematic stratigraphy of site UA 53 showing the relationship between different cultural and climatic phases, as well as the environmental factors affecting the site formation processes; the soil eroded when arid conditions prevailed is highlighted by the gray colour.

In this dynamically changing environment, it was hypothesized that the change in the course of the Gash river also affected the region and its inhabitants. Actually, it was suggested that the course of the Gash river, thought to have originally reached the Atbara, may have progressively moved north up to its present location, and that the streams crossing the region between the Gash and the Atbara rivers may be palaeo-channels of the Gash (see e.g. Sadr 1991: 33, Fig. 3.7) (Figures 5, 6 f). But this model does not seem to be supported by recent investigations, and the streams previously considered as palaeo-channels of the Gash are now interpreted as autonomous water courses, most likely already crossing the region in ancient times.[1] Indeed, the above described thick sediment strata covering at a certain point some of the archaeological sites of the region like UA 50 and UA 53 may have been originated by the action of those streams prevailing in more humid phases on the wind erosion (Manzo 2015: 235).

1.4 The resources

In addition to agricultural land and grazing areas, that represented the basic resources sustaining the subsistence economy of the region, Eastern Sudan is also extremely rich in minerals, vegetation and animal resources relevant for the ancient trade. Other resources are also occurring just southeast and south of the region, on the slopes of the Ethio-Eritrean highlands. This makes the Eastern Sudan and the Eritrean lowlands traditionally crucial for the supply of commodities such as African ebony, ivory, aromatic resins and even gold, all available in the region or its immediate vicinity (Manzo 1999: 6-9, 13) (Figure 9).

A large variety of plant and animal species occur in the number of rich and different ecological niches characterizing the slopes and the foothills of the Ethio-Eritrean highlands, mainly due to the variation in altitude and in the availability of water. Actually, in terms of animal resources, ostriches, whose feathers and eggshell were both appreciated in ancient times, widely occurred in Eastern Sudan as well as in more northern regions up to the beginning of the last century (Dardano and Riccardi 1936: 20-21; Mackworth-Praed and Grant 1981: 1-3; Munzinger 1890: 104; see also Phillips 2000: 332). Also, giraffes (Dardano and Riccardi 1936: 20-21; Grasse 1955: 606) and leopards (Corbet 1978: 71; Maydon 1924), that may have provided prized animal skins (see Osborn and Osbornová 1998: 121, 150; Van Driel-Murray 2000: 302), but could also be traded alive already in very ancient times, as shown in several Egyptian scenes representing the paying of tribute by foreign lands south of Egypt (see e.g. Osborn and Osbornová 1998: 150-151), were common in Eastern Sudan up to very recent times. Although extinct today in the region, the rhino too occurred there and certainly was also present in ancient times (Dardano and Riccardi 1936: 20-21; Grasse 1955: 1123-1126; Osborn and Osbornová 1998: 139-140). On the contrary, baboons that were exported to Egypt as pets as well as for their religious significance (Osborn and Osbornová 1998: 35-36, 39) still occur in Eastern Sudan (Corbet 1978: 65; Osborn and Osbornová 1998: 33, 38). Elephants provided ivory, but were also needed alive in the 3rd-early 2nd century BC, and despite their heavy exploitation, occurred in Eastern Sudan well after the mid-19th century (Maydon 1924; Munzinger 1890: 100-104; see also Krzyszowska and Morkot 2000: 323-326; Osborn and Osbornová 1998: 126).

Eastern Sudan and in general the lower slopes of the Ethio-Eritrean highlands are characterized by the occurrence of several plant species highly appreciated in ancient times, both for the production of furniture and for aromatic resins. Both *Boswellia* spp. (Hepper 1969; Manetti 1936: 104; Scaweinfurth 1891; Serpico 2000: 438-439) and *Commiphora* (Hepper 1969; Manetti 1936: 168; Scaweinfurth 1891; Serpico 2000: 439-442), exploited for the aromatic substances originating from their resin, occur in the region. Other plant species such as *Dalbergia melonoxylon* and *Dyospiros mespiliformis*, whose hard and dark brown or black wood was appreciated since ancient times for the production of furniture, inlay, veneer and sculpture (see Gale *et al.* 2000: pp. 338-340), occur in the region, where they were exploited up to recent times (Booth

---

[1] M. Cremaschi is in charge of these investigations. These remarks are based on the preliminary results of his analyses.

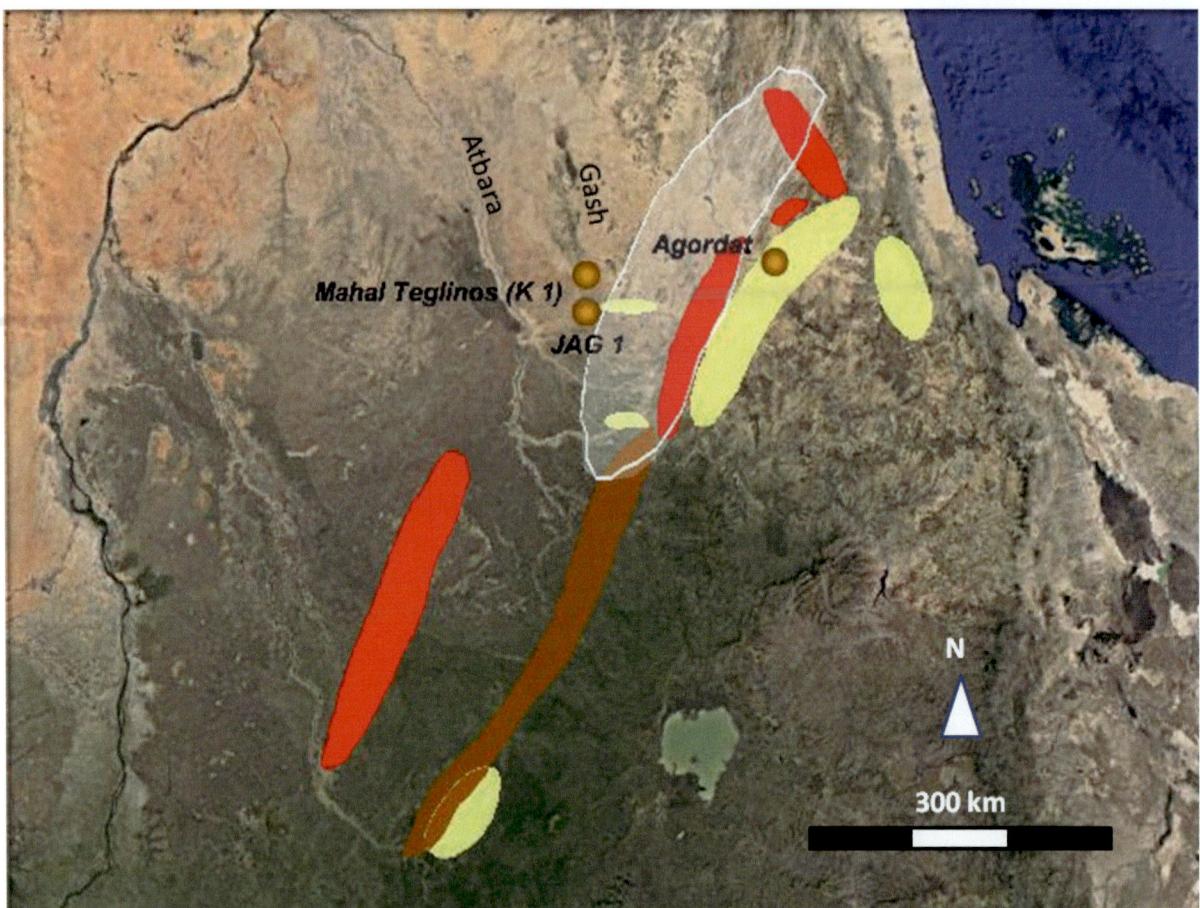

FIGURE 9: MAP SHOWING THE OCCURRENCE OF RAW MATERIALS IN THE REGION AND NEARBY AS WELL AS THE MAIN ARCHAEOLOGICAL SITES; AROMATIC RESINS OCCUR IN THE AREAS HIGHLIGHTED IN RED, EBONY IN THE BROWN ONES, GOLD IN THE YELLOW ONES, WHILE WHITE COLOUR SHOWS WHERE ELEPHANTS WERE RECORDED WELL AFTER THE MID-19TH CENTURY (BASED ON FATTOVICH 1991D).

1952; Scaweinfurth 1891).

As far as mineral resources are concerned, generally the region on both sides of the present Sudanese-Eritrean border, and in particular in the basin of the Gash river is characterized by the occurrence of gold sources, as well as by traces of their possible ancient exploitation (Whiteman 1971: 224-225 see also Ogden 2000: 161-162). Other prized mineral resources such as agate, chalcedony and cornelian, highly appreciated in ancient times for the production of beads and jewelry (see e.g. Aston, Harrell and Shaw 2000: 25-26), are naturally present in the gravels of the Atbara (Whiteman 1971: 257-258).

1.5 Communications

As emphasized earlier, Eastern Sudan is located between several different eco-cultural regions of northeastern Africa such as the Eastern Desert and the Red Sea hills, the middle Nile valley, the Butana and the Ethio-Eritrean highlands. Therefore, the region is traditionally crossed by routes linking these different areas. Actually, given the above described great ecological diversity of the region, and the seasonal variability in the availability of resources, periodical displacements and migrations of animals -including human beings- took place since the earliest times. Moreover, the above described availability of appreciated raw materials in the region itself and in its immediate environs may have also favored the development and utilization of an articulated network of tracks (Manzo 1999: 12-13).

In general, it should be remarked that the mobility within Eastern Sudan, and between it and the neighboring regions, was facilitated by the availability of water due to the monsoon rains affecting the area, a crucial factor even in drier climatic phases (see above 1.3 *Present and past environment*). Nevertheless, it should also be remarked that on the other hand, the rainy season may also have posed periodical problems to mobility, such as the formation of muddy areas, pools and the increased water level in rivers with the consequent difficulties in wading across the Atbara and the Gash (James 1867: 49-50; Munzinger 1890: 25).

As previously mentioned, the emergence of some specific routes was perhaps facilitated precisely by the seasonal availability of resources such as water and grass. The areas closer to the slopes of the Ethio-Eritrean highlands along the southeastern and southern fringes of Eastern Sudan, and the ones near the rivers are characterized by a constant availability of resources throughout the year, while the central part of the region is mainly characterized by a concentration of resources in summer and immediately after it, as their availability is related to the seasonal monsoon rains. Therefore, the location of the Atbara and the Gash respectively on the western and eastern fringes of the region may have determined east-west movements from the rivers to the inner part of the region and vice versa. Nevertheless, it should be remarked that the occurrence of badly eroded terraces and very poor soils along the Atbara may have limited the use of that area as shelter in the dry season, at least from a certain point onwards. On the other hand, the north-south, or more precisely north/west-south/east movements may have been favored by the presence of the Ethio-Eritrean highlands to the south and south-east of the region, and in this case the movements also had to overcome some differences in altitude. Finally, to the north, the region is open towards the Eastern Desert, and no clear-cut ecological borders are marked by rivers or altitude. North of the region, in the Eastern Desert itself, a not less relevant invisible line is marked around latitude 22° N (this may have fluctuated in the different climatic phases): two climatic zones, one characterized by winter rains to the north and the other affected by summer rains to the south meet there (Bintliff and Barnard 2012: 438; see also Barbour 1961: 38). This invisible line was crossed two times every year in opposite directions by several animal species -also in this case including man- to exploit the resources available north and south of it in different periods of the year, due to the two opposite climatic regimes. Some of these north-south movements may have extended up to the northern fringes of Eastern Sudan.

As far as the main known tracks and routes traditionally used by the caravans and often in the seasonal movements of the livestock breeders are concerned, some of them put our region in communication with the Red Sea coast and the Ethio-Eritrean highlands. Towards the sea, those tracks, also used by Muslim pilgrims, point to the north-east and lead to the coast near Aidab, Swakin and, later into the sector of the littoral where Port Sudan is located (Hurst 1952: 87; James 1867: 112-116; Monneret de Villard 1938). A further track to the north-east reached the coast through Maman and the valley of the Barca river (Monneret de Villard 1938).

Other tracks pointing to the south and south-east reached the highlands by crossing the area between the Gash and the Barka: the valley of the Gash there may have represented a natural corridor to the highlands (Maydon 1924; Morrice 1949). A further track, through Metemma and following in part the Atbara, also leads to the highlands (James 1867: 112-116; Maydon 1924).

From the region of Kassala, some tracks heading to the north-west reached the Butana by crossing the Atbara at the ford of Goz Regeb and were connected through it to the wide network of tracks crossing the Butana, following the Nile and also crossing the Bayuda to avoid the big meander of the Nile (Hurst 1952: 76-77; Morrice 1949; Monneret de Villard 1938).

Thus, if the previously outlined natural factors may have determined periodical north-south and east-west movements in the region, specific routes emerged from the distribution of the watering points, of the passes overcoming hills, and of fords where the rivers could be crossed or simply from more economic, i.e. less energy consuming, itineraries. Of course, this does not exclude the possibility of other factors affecting the development of the network of routes, and also the abandonment of some of them in certain moments: these are mainly represented by socio-economic circumstances. Some of these circumstances will emerge in the following chapters.

Chapter 2
The emerging of a regional tradition (c. 6000-3000 BC)

2.1 The Pre-Saroba sites and the Amm Adam Group

It should be emphasized right from the very beginning that what is described in this chapter is not the earliest evidence of human presence recorded in Eastern Sudan. Actually, some Lower to Middle Paleolithic sites are located on the western bank of the Atbara, associated with Pleistocene gravels and gave chert chopping tools apparently in association with bones of elephants, rhinoceros, antelope and gazelle (Cremaschi *et al.* 1986: 47-48; Shiner *et al.* 1971: 296, 306-308). Not far from them, a site dated to 10000-6000 years ago on the basis of the typology of its stone tools -mainly geometrics, blades, and truncations on blades- and two further sites with different lithic assemblages -mainly scrapers, burins on flakes, pointed blades with some microliths- were recorded (Shiner *et al.* 1971: 308-316). Nevertheless, the lack of a systematic study of these Paleolithic phases, so far recorded only in the region immediately west of the Atbara, prevents us from understanding if and eventually how they contributed to the emergence of the earliest ceramic phase of the region, which was labeled as Pre-Saroba.

The chronology of this phase is based on a couple of radiocarbon dates[2] suggesting that the Pre-Saroba sites may go back to the second half of the 6th millennium BC.

This phase was characterized by two different groups of sites with distinctive traits in terms of material culture. The first group, located in the northern Gash delta, was specifically labeled as Amm Adam Group, while a second group, simply referred to as Pre-Saroba sites, was recorded in the area of Khashm el-Girba (Marks and Fattovich 1989: 453-454; Fattovich 1989a: 481-484, 1990a: 11-13; Fattovich, Marks and Mohammed Ali 1984: 178; Manzo *et al.* 2012: 47-50; Marks 1987: 90; Marks and Sadr 1988: 74; see also Fattovich 1991a: 95-97). The sites near Khashm el-Girba were characterized by impressed ceramics recalling those occurring in the Mesolithic assemblages in the Nile valley, with only some examples of knobbed ware, a very distinctive type of pottery characterizing the regional tradition, whose surfaces were typically covered by knobs and with cylindrical cavities in the wall of the vessel in correspondence with the knob (Figure 10 a), a prevailing type of decoration in the sites of the Gash delta. In particular, the sites dating back to this phase surveyed in 2010 and 2011 between Gash and Atbara, and not far from the cluster previously recorded in

FIGURE 10: FRAGMENTS OF PRE-SAROBA CERAMICS: A) SHERD FROM A KNOBBED WARE VESSEL FROM SITE UA 72; B) SHERD WITH ROCKER STAMP PACKED DECORATION FROM SITE UA 72; C) SHERD WITH INCISED WAVY LINE DECORATION FROM SITE UA 42 (SCALE IN CM).

---
[2] SMU 1139: 6215±75 bp; Beta 437225: 6090±30 bp.

the Khashm el-Girba sector, gave ceramics related to the Mesolithic in the Nile valley characterized by impressed decorations similar to the rocker stamp packed (Figure 10 b), and possibly incised wavy line (Figure 10 c), impressed wavy line, as well as rare fragments of knobbed ware (Manzo *et al.* 2012: 47-50, see also Fattovich 1990a: 11-12).

The occurrence of sherds in the Nile valley sites of the Khartoum region characterized by dotted wavy line decoration, together with sherds with incised wavy lines in assemblages dating to the beginning of the Mesolithic period (Salvatori 2012: 412-414; Usai 2016: 13) may suggest that some dotted wavy line sherds occurring in the surface collections of Pre-Saroba sites of Eastern Sudan, where they are sometimes associated with materials typical of the Pre-Saroba phase, may also date to this phase in our region. Of course, also in Eastern Sudan the impressed wavy line sherds cannot be any more automatically regarded as later than the incised wavy line ones.

Interestingly, in the Nile valley some sherds with scraped surfaces were recorded in Mesolithic assemblages dating from the early 7th millennium BC and are increasingly frequent in the mid-7th millennium BC, according to the newly established ceramic sequence of the sites of the Khartoum region (Salvatori 2012: 416). As scraped sherds were also collected at some Pre-Saroba and Amm Adam Group sites (Fattovich 1989a: 484, 1990a: 12, 1991a: 97), the fresh evidence coming from the Nile valley may suggest that the association between the Pre-Saroba knobbed and impressed wares and scraped sherds could not be due to post-depositional processes, or to the mixing of materials from different phases on the surface of the sites, and may even push back the beginning of the regional Atbai Ceramic Tradition, precisely characterized by the scraped ware, to this specific phase. As already remarked (Fattovich 1990a: 13; Fattovich, Marks and Mohammed Ali 1984: 178), the occurrence of the knobbed ware both in Pre-Saroba sites and in Saroba sites of the Malawiya Group too may support this hypothesis of continuity in the development of the regional ceramic tradition since Pre-Saroba times, which needs of course to be confirmed with further specific investigations. Moreover, despite the fact that the hypothesis of a local development in Eastern Sudan of the scraped ware from the incised wavy line cannot certainly be discarded, the occurrence of sherds with scraped surfaces in Mesolithic sites of the Nile valley may also support the idea that the origin of the most typical feature of the regional ceramic tradition of Eastern Sudan may actually be in the Nile valley.

The lithic industry of this phase is characterized by a large number of blade tools, while chert and agate were the preferred raw materials (Marks 1987: 90).

As far as the distribution of the sites throughout the region is concerned (Figure 11), as previously mentioned, the Pre-Saroba phase is characterized by two distinct groups of sites apparently with

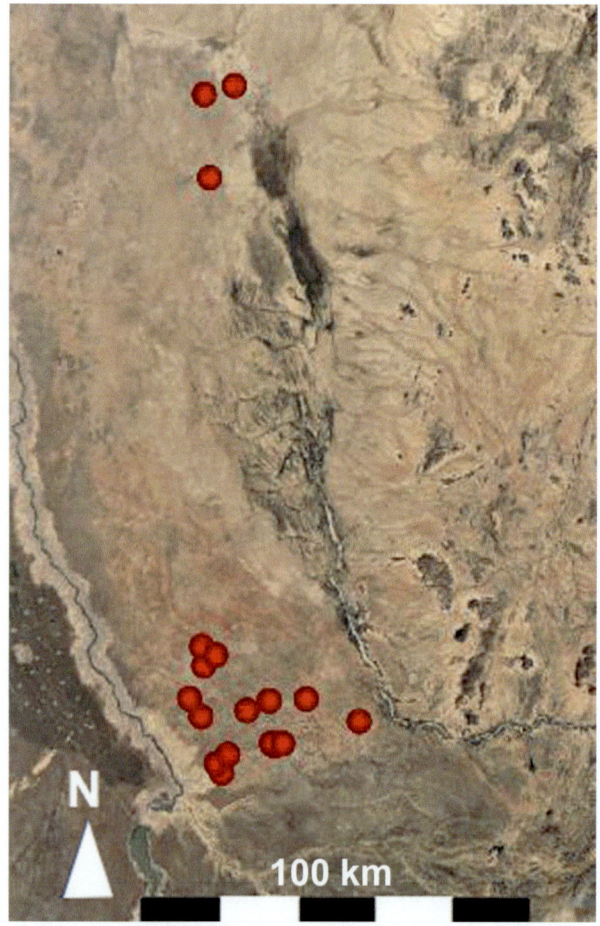

FIGURE 11: MAP SHOWING THE DISTRIBUTION OF THE PRE-SAROBA SITES (PLOTTED ON GOOGLE EARTH SATELLITE IMAGE).

some distinctive traits in terms of material culture and located in the Gash delta -the Amm Adam Group- and near Khashm el-Girba (Fattovich 1989a: 484, 1990a: 11, 1991a: 95; Marks and Fattovich 1989: 453-454; Fattovich, Marks and Mohammed Ali 1984: 178). Nevertheless, the alleged lack of Pre-Saroba sites in the area between Gash and Atbara (Fattovich 1989a: 484; Fattovich, Marks and Mohammed Ali 1984: 178; Marks and Fattovich 1989: 454) should be reconsidered in light of the recent discoveries of Pre-Saroba sites located not only in the vicinity of Khor Marmadeb, but also in the steppe, east of the Atbara river (Manzo *et al.* 2012: 43). This fact seems to show a broader distribution of the Pre-Saroba sites, somehow confirming what was previously suggested on the basis of the occurrence of two possible Amm Adam Group sites located between the delta of the Gash river and the Atbara, close to Jebel el Ukheiderat and Jebel Ofreik (Fattovich 1991a: 95).

The available information on the adaptive systems adopted in this phase were provided mainly by Amm Adam Group sites in the Gash delta and are very limited: they consist of evidence of impressions of grains of unspecified small seeded grass and Millet sp. on ceramics (Alemseged Beldados 2015: 74-75, 79-80, Table 8.2) (Table 1), and of archaeozoological remains of buffalo, hippopotamus, grazing antelopes and fish, suggesting the exploitation of animals typical of a humid environment (Geerards 1983) (Table 2). A late Pre-Saroba shell midden radiocarbon dated to *c.* 5000 BC recently excavated at site UA 50 consisted mainly of remains of land snails (Manzo 2016: 194, Fig. 7) (Figure 12). All of this, provisionally suggests an economic model based on the exploitation of wild animal and plant species available in a more humid environment (see also Fattovich 1990a: 13), also coherent with the general palaeoenvironmental setting of northeastern Africa and of this specific region in this phase, as well as with the location of the sites near the streams crossing the area between the Gash and the Atbara rivers in the southern sector of the region and in the Gash delta in the north.

Group/Phase	Chronology	Site(s)	Species
Amm Adam Group	6th mill. BC	Amm Adam Station (site 1), Eriba Station (site 2)	Unspecified millet
Malawiya Group	5th mill. BC		No data
Butana Group	4th-early 3rd mill. BC	Khasm el Girba (sites 23 and 96), UA 14	*Panicum* sp., *Setaria* sp., *Echinochloa* sp., *Sorghum* sp., *Hordeum* sp., *Triticum* sp.
Gash Group	Early 3rd-early 2nd mill. BC	Kassala (site 1)	*Hordeum* sp., *Triticum* sp., *Sorghum bicolor bicolor*, *Sorghum verticilliflorum*, *Panicum* sp., *Eleusine* sp., *Phalaris* sp., *Ziziphus spina-christi*, *Celtis integrifolia*, *Vigna unguiculata*, *Grewia bicolor* Juss, *Echinochloa* sp., *Setaria* sp., *Adansonia digitata*
Jebel Mokram Group	Early 2nd mill. BC-early 1st mill BC	Kassala (site 1), Jebel Mokram (site 2), EG (site 3), Jebel Abu Gamal (site 1), Shurab el Gash (site 9), UA53	*Sorghum bicolor bicolor*, *Panicum* sp., *Pennisetum* sp., *Eleusine* sp., *Setaria* sp., *Vigna unguiculata*, *Ziziphus* sp., *Lolium* sp., *Eleusine* sp.
Hagiz Group	Early 1st mill. BC-1st mill. AD	Shurab el Gash (site 42), UA129	*Panicum* sp., *Eleusine* sp., *Sorghum bicolor bicolor*
Gergaf Group	AD 15th-18th cent.	UA 126	*Sorghum* sp., *Panicum* sp., unspecified millet

TABLE 1: PLANT SPECIES IDENTIFIED IN ARCHAEOLOGICAL ASSEMBLAGES FROM EASTERN SUDAN.

Group/Phase	Chronology	Site	Species
Amm Adam Group	6th mill. BC	Amm Adam Station (site 1), Eriba Station (sites 2, 3, 4)	Unspecified antelopes, *Syncerus cafer*, *Hippopotamus amphibius*, *Achatina fulica*, *Pila ovata*
Malawiya Group	5th mill. BC	Various unspecified sites	Unspecified antelopes, land snails
Butana Group	4th-early 3rd mill. BC	UA 53, Khashm el Girba (sites 23, 29)	*Achatina fulica, Pila ovata, Pila wernei, Lanistes carinatus, Limicolaria cailliaudi, Hippopotamus amphibius, Phacocerus aethiopicus, Bos primigenius*, unspecified caprovines
Gash Group	Early 3rd-early 2nd mill. BC	Kassala (site 1)	*Pila wernei, Lanistes carinatus, Limicolaria cailliaudi, Spathopsis wahlbergi/rubens, Clarias* sp., *Synodontis* sp., Tilapiini, *Protopterus aethiopicus, Polypterus* sp., *Cercopithecus guereza, Felix caracal, Canidae* sp., *Redunca redunca, Kobus kob, Tragelaphus strepsiceros, Varanus niloticus, Python sebae, Strutio camelus, Numida meleagris, Lepus capensis, Canis aureus, Vulpes ruppellii, Orycteropus afer, Procavia capensis, Phacocerus aethiopicus, Syncerus cafer, Gazella rufifrons/dorcas, Madoqua saltiana, Canis familiaris, Equus africanus, Bos primigenius*, Rodentia, unspecified caprovines, birds and antelopes
Jebel Mokram Group	Early 2nd mill. BC-early 1st mill BC	Kassala (site 1), Khashm el Girba (site 20)	*Mutela dubia, Spathopsis wahlbergi/rubens, Clarias* sp., *Synodontis* sp., Tilapiini, Chelonia, *Numida meleagris, Syncerus cafer, Gazella rufifrons/dorcas, Madoqua saltiana, Equus africanus, Bos primigenius*, unspecified birds, antelopes and caprovines
Hagiz Group	Early 1st mill. BC-1st mill. AD	Various sites	*Bos primigenius*, unspecified caprovines

TABLE 2: ANIMAL SPECIES IDENTIFIED IN ARCHAEOLOGICAL ASSEMBLAGES FROM EASTERN SUDAN.

2.2 The Malawiya Group

This badly known culture was defined on the basis of finds from some sites in the steppe between Gash and Atbara characterized by ceramics with rocker comb impressed decoration generically reminiscent of the Khartoum Horizon Style (Fattovich 1989a: 486, 1990a: 13, 1991a: 97-98; Marks and Fattovich 1989: 455; see also Marks and Sadr 1988: 74; Shiner *et al.* 1971: 317-334, Fig. 5 a-b). Several sites to be ascribed to this culture were also recorded in the same area in 2010 and 2011 (Manzo *et al.* 2012: 43) (Figure 13).

The absolute chronology of the Malawiya Group is based only on a couple of radiocarbon dates suggesting a date of around the mid 5th millennium BC for this culture.[3]

In particular, the pottery is characterized by rocker alternated pivoted stamp impressed decorative patterns (Figure 14 a), a feature already occurring in the Late Mesolithic but mainly related to the Neolithic phase in the Nile valley (Salvatori 2012: 416), and by spaced rocker comb impressed patterns,

---

[3] Marks and Sadr 1988: 73, SMU 1285: 5632±66 bp, SMU 1181: 5644±70 bp.

FIGURE 12: LATE PRE-SAROBA SHELL MIDDEN AT SITE UA 50.

also similar to the ones recorded in the Neolithic sites in the Nile valley (Figure 14 b). Moreover, a more accurate type of knobbed ware associated on the surface of some sites with Malawiya Group materials can perhaps be ascribed to this culture (Fattovich, Marks and Mohammed Ali 1984: 178; Fattovich 1990a: 13) (Figure 14 c).

The lithic industry was a blade one, and in terms of tools characterized by denticulates and lunates, occasionally by scrapers and notches, while the preferred raw material was chert, although the use of agate and quartz was remarked as well (Shiner *et al.* 1971: 317-332, Fig. 4, 6, 7). Apparently, grinding stones were common in the assemblages of this phase (Marks and Sadr 1988: 72; Shiner *et al.* 1971: 325).

Although no systematic investigation was conducted on the adaptive system of this culture, it was remarked that bones of different species of antelopes as well as shells of land snails characterized the Malawiya Group sites, nevertheless the occurrence of land snails may be natural and related to the life cycle of these gastropods as it was remarked that their operculum is still in place, and this may suggest that they were not extracted for consumption (Marks and Sadr 1988: 74-75 (Table 2). This scanty archaeozoological evidence, together with the occurrence of some grinding stones and the location of the Malawiya Group sites, mostly far from the Atbara and absent in the Gash delta, may suggest that, although the exploitation of humid environment near the streams crossing the steppe and perhaps the Atbara itself continued, a major emphasis was placed on the exploitation of the animals and plants available in the steppe itself. Actually the limited dimensions of some sites as well as the un-existing depth of the deposits have already been remarked by Shiner who suggested that some of the sites of this phase located in the steppe may have been seasonal camps (Shiner *et al.* 1971: 323 see also Fattovich 1990a: 13-14).

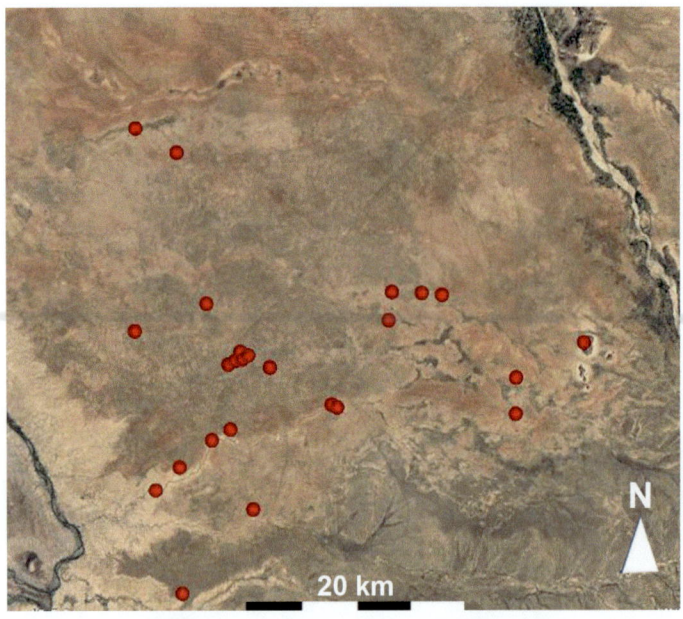

FIGURE 13: MAP SHOWING THE DISTRIBUTION OF THE MALAWIYA GROUP SITES (PLOTTED ON GOOGLE EARTH SATELLITE IMAGE).

FIGURE 14: FRAGMENTS OF MALAWIYA GROUP CERAMICS: A) ALTERNATED PIVOTED STAMP DECORATED SHERD FROM SITE UA 48; B) SPACED ROCKER STAMP DECORATED SHERD FROM SITE UA 18; C) RIM SHERD OF A KNOBBED WARE BOWL FROM SITE UA 18 (SCALE IN CM).

2.3 The Butana Group

The absolute chronology of this culture may correspond to the 4th-early 3rd millennium BC, as suggested by several available radiocarbon dates,[4] and also in agreement with a couple of radiocarbon dates from the earliest occupation phase at Mahal Teglinos (K 1), to be ascribed to an eastern variant of the Butana Group.[5]

The pottery of this phase is characterized by rims with incised herringbone bands on the lip (Figure 15 a), fingernail impressed sherds, restricted orifice bowls with incised or impressed external decoration (Figure 15 b), often consisting of herringbone patterns (Figure 15 c), scraped vessels with pinched or impressed indented rim (Figure 15 e), burnished patterns, rippled ware and black topped ware, often with parallel rows of notches on the external surface (Figure 15 d) (Fattovich 1989a: 487, 1990a: 14,1991a: 99; Fattovich, Marks and Mohammed Ali 1984: 179-180; Manzo et al. 2011: 5, 2012: 52-55; Marks and Fattovich 1989: 455; Sadr 1991: 38; Shiner et al. 1971: 346-348, Fig. 11 a-b, 356-358, 365-368, Fig. 15-16, 375-377, Fig. 19 a-b, 379-381, 387-389, Fig. 22, a; Winchell 2013: 148-192).

Interestingly, the Butana Group ceramic materials can be compared generically to the Late Neolithic pottery of the Nile valley and more specifically to the Pre-Kerma Upper Nubian ceramic assemblages because of the big bowls with incised decoration on the thickened lip, the rippled ware, the continuous edge rocker decorations on the walls of the vessels

---

[4] See Marks and Sadr 1988: 73: SMU 1156: 4421±93 bp, SMU 1151: 4569±69 bp, SMU 1188: 4519±67 bp, SMU 1155: 4542±253 bp, SMU 1201: 4727±154 bp; Shiner et al. 1971: 381: TX 445: 4410±90 bp; Manzo et al. 2012: 8, 15: Beta 311300: 5010±30 bp, Beta 311302: 5080±30 bp; still unpublished dates: Beta 437223: 5004±30, Beta 437224: 4560±30.
[5] Fattovich 1993: 246: Gif 7654: 4220±90 bp, and unpublished date GX 18105: 4900±170 bp.

Figure 15: fragments of Butana Group ceramics: a) rim of a bowl with incised herringbone band on the lip from site UA 113; b) rim of a restricted orifice bowl with rocker impressed external decoration from site KG 23/UA 14; c) wall sherd of a bowl with herringbone incised decoration on the external surface from site KG 23/UA 14; d) rim of a black topped ware cup with parallel rows of notches on the external surface from site KG 23/UA 14; e) rim of a scraped vessel with impressions on the lip from site UA 113 (scale in cm).

(Manzo 2014b: 1152-1153; Manzo et al. 2011: 5), while a complete small bag-shaped brown ware flask with burnished external surfaces from site UA 53 is reminiscent of a bottle from Kadruka or of A-Group types (Figure 16 a), and a fragmentary conical large bowl with a vertical rim always from UA 53 (Figure 16 b) is similar to shapes from Pre-Kerma but also A-Group Nubian assemblages (Manzo et al. 2012: 55). These similarities with the Late Neolithic of the Nile valley and in particular with the Pre-Kerma Upper Nubian materials show that the Butana Group fits well into the general 4th and early 3rd millennium BC cultural framework of Nubia and Sudan, also in agreement with the absolute chronology suggested for the Butana Group by the radiocarbon dates.

The Butana Group lithic industries consisted of bipolar cores and flakes, with some crescents, double perforators, denticulated scrapers and backed pieces, and very typical chipped stone picks (Figure 17), while as far as the raw materials are concerned, chert and flint are more frequent than agate (Shiner et al. 1971: 335-394, Fig. 9-10, 13-14, 17-18, 20-21; Winchell 2013: 14). The recent excavations at UA 53 also broaden our knowledge of the Butana Group lithic industries, with collections apparently corresponding

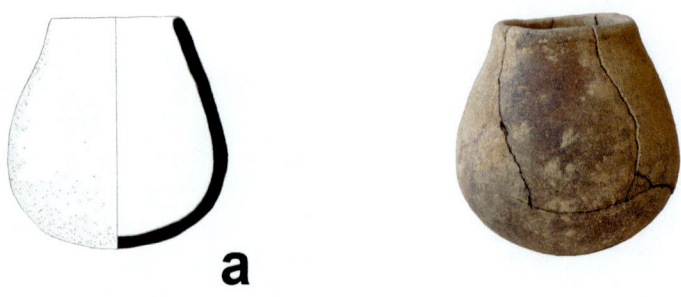

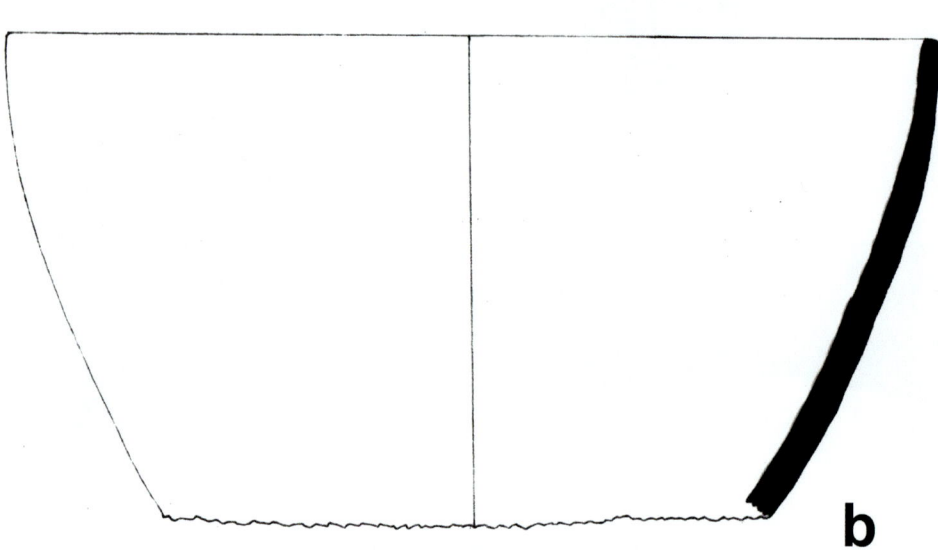

Figure 16: a) complete Butana Group flask from site UA 53 excavation unit VI; b) fragmentary Butana Group large conical bowl from site UA 53 excavation unit IV (scale in cm).

Figure 17: Butana Group chipped stone pick from site KG 23/UA 14 (scale in cm).

to the descriptions made after the earlier investigations of Butana Group sites in the area close to the Atbara (Manzo et al. 2012: 85-86): the collection there mainly consists of debitage resulting from single platform cores, while crescents, double backed perforators, denticulates/scrapers and backed pieces are the only tools, and the exploited raw materials were flint/chert and agate.

Test-excavations were conducted in the Seventies and the Eighties in several Butana Group sites near Khashm el-Girba (KG 28B, considered as a transition site between the Malawiya and the Butana Groups, N 101, N 107, N 123, KG 23, KG 27; KG 29, KG 1, KG 96, and KG 5) (Winchell 2013: 17-21, 192-210, see also Shiner *et al.* 1971: 335-370) and at Mahal Teglinos (K 1), where the earliest occupation phase in the central sector of the site can be ascribed to a local variant of this culture, there also labeled as Proto-Gash (Fattovich 1989b: 227-228, 1991a: 99, 1993a: 263; Fattovich, Sadr and Vitagliano 1988-1989: 338; Fattovich and Vitagliano 1987: 57). At Mahal Teglinos (K 1), the so far only evidence of the structures associated with a Butana Group settlement was recovered: it consists of circular or sub-rectangular post holes marking the perimeter of two possible rounded huts, built side to side and showing traces of three possible phases of rebuilding (Fattovich, Manzo and Usai 1994: 15). In more recent years excavations were conducted at UA 53, an early Butana Group site along the Khor Marmadeb, in the southern sector of the investigated area, between the Atbara and the Gash rivers, but no evidence of structures was brought to light there except for some pits filled with stones, whose purpose is still to be clarified (Manzo *et al.* 2012: 6-21; Manzo 2013: 257-259; 2014a: 379-382).

These excavations also provided elements on the economy of this culture, which apparently relied on wild game like antelopes, but also suidae and elephants, as well as on fish, fresh water shellfish and land snails, especially in the earlier phases (Peters 1989, 1992; Manzo *et al.* 2012: 94-95), and also on livestock in the later phases (Peters 1989, 1992, see also Marks and Sadr 1988: 78), when great emphasis was apparently placed on the exploitation of cattle and the ovicaprids, as livestock also become quantitatively dominant in the archaeozoological assemblage (Gautier and Van Neer 2006: Tab. 1) (Tables 2-4). At site UA 53, several shell middens dating to the early 4th millennium BC and most likely originated by the intensive exploitation of land snails were investigated (Manzo *et al.* 2012: 7-9, 15; Manzo 2013: 259, 2014: 379-380) (Figure 18). In the meantime, in Butana Group times, domesticated wheat and barley as well as morphologically wild sorghum and millet were exploited (D'Andrea and Tsubakisaka 1990; Alemseged Beldados 2015: 79-80, Table 8.2) (Table 1).

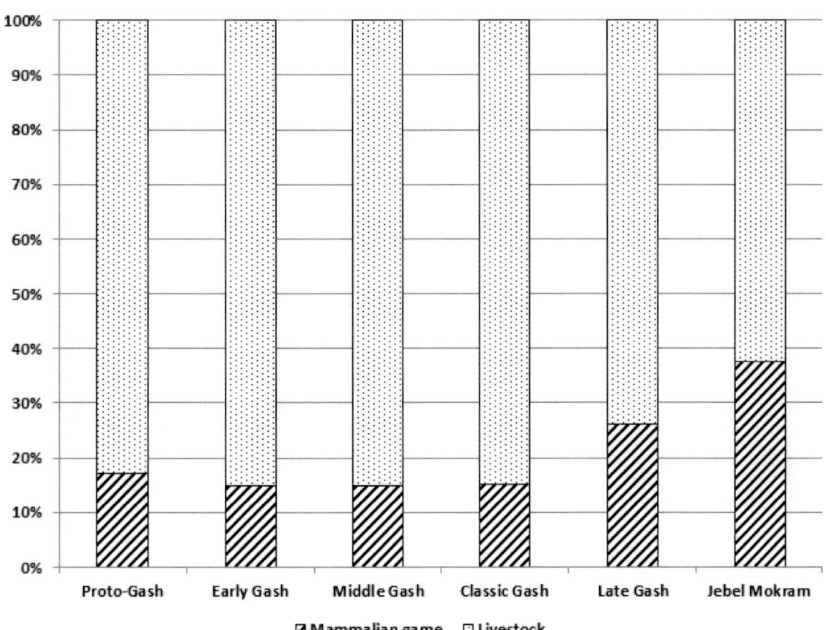

TABLE 3: FREQUENCY OF WILD AND DOMESTICATED MAMMALIANS IN ARCHAEOLOGICAL ASSEMBLAGES FROM EASTERN SUDAN.

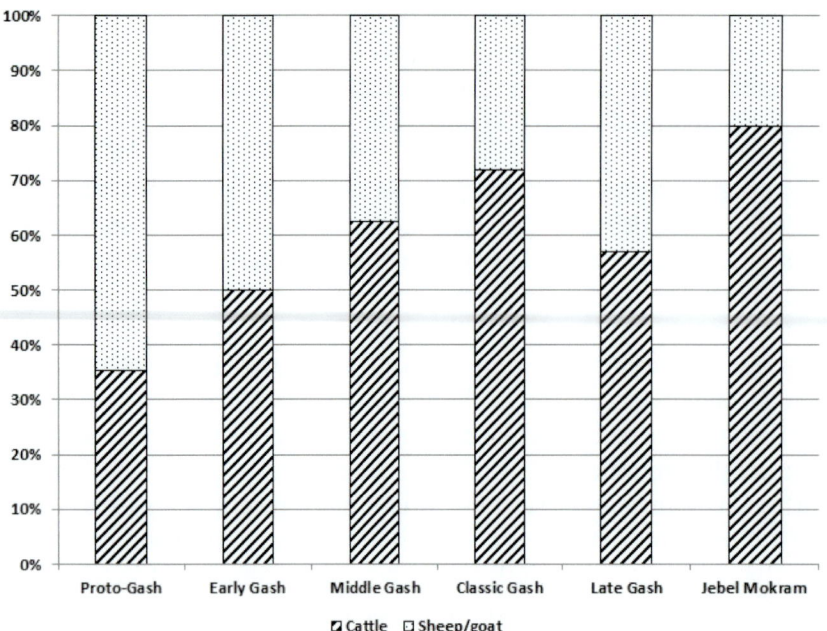

Table 4: frequency of cattle and sheep/goat in archaeological assemblages from Eastern Sudan.

Figure 18: early Butana Group shell midden in excavation unit XI at site UA 53.

The settlement pattern of the Butana Group is characterized by the occurrence of some large settlement sites -the largest one is KG 23/UA 14, exceeding 10 hectares- some with thick stratified deposit suggesting a prolonged, or at least a repeated occupation, close to the Atbara and in the steppe between the Atbara and the Gash rivers, along the streams crossing that area, while some smaller sites with thinner deposit and low artifact density are located around the major settlements and, more sparsely, in the eastern sector of the region, where large settlements are apparently absent (Fattovich 1989a: 487-488, 1990a: 14, 1991a: 98; Fattovich, Marks and Mohammed Ali 1984: 179-180; Fattovich, Sadr and Vitagliano 1988-1989: 337; Manzo et al. 2012: 44; Marks and Fattovich 1989: 455; Marks and Sadr 1988: 75-76; Sadr 1988: 391, 394-395, 1991: 38; see also Shiner et al. 1971: 350, 359, 370)

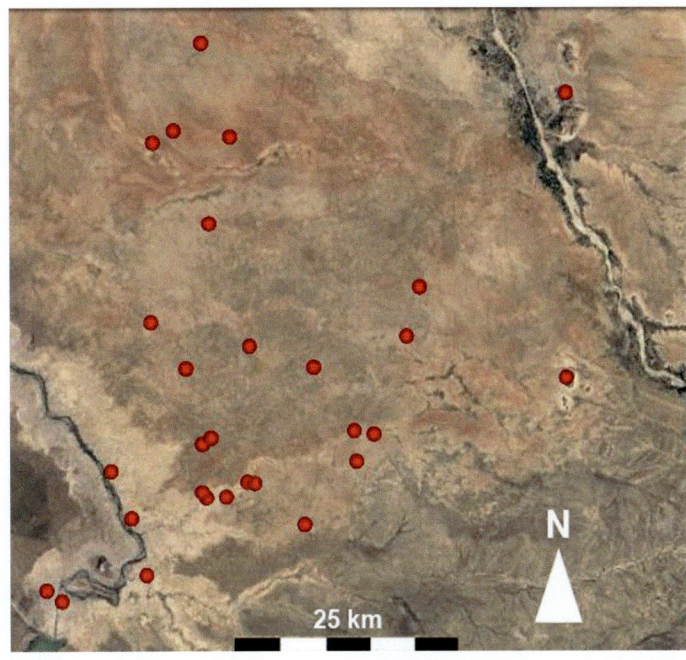

FIGURE 19: MAP SHOWING THE DISTRIBUTION OF THE BUTANA GROUP SITES (PLOTTED ON GOOGLE EARTH SATELLITE IMAGE).

(Figure 19). Not only the dimensions and the thick stratified deposit of some sites, but also the above described evidence suggesting the rebuilding of huts at Mahal Teglinos (K 1) support the hypothesis that some of the Butana Group sites were at least repeatedly occupied. The features of the settlement pattern of the Butana Group also seem coherent with an adaptive strategy based on the exploitation of the wet environment near the rivers and, from a certain point onwards, on agro-pastoralism. Interestingly, some of the so far investigated sites may have had specialized functions, like in the case of KG 50, possibly a lithic production site (Winchell 2013: 17; see also Marks and Sadr 1988: 77), N 125, perhaps a ceramic production site (Winchell 2013: 17; Shiner et al. 1971: 379-381), while UA 53 may have been a seasonal camp specialized in the exploitation of land snails in early Butana Group times (Manzo et al. 2012: 103; Manzo 2013: 257, 259, 2014a: 386).

Very few data are available for the Butana Group funerary customs. Only a late Butana Group cemetery, dating to the last centuries of the 4th millennium BC, was recorded and partially investigated in recent years at site UA 53 (Manzo et al. 2012: 7; Manzo 2014a: 380-382, 2015: 233-234): no traces of superstructures, possibly destroyed by erosion like the upper part of the funerary pits, were recorded, while the bodies lied in contracted position with different orientations, and with grave goods consisting only of personal ornaments, mainly lip plugs (Figure 20), but also ornaments made from Red Sea shells (Figure 21). Interestingly, in other Butana Group sites it was remarked that personal ornaments as well as mace heads were often made of exotic stones such as basalt, possibly originating from as far as the Red Sea hills (Marks and Sadr 1988: 72, 76; Sadr 1991: 38; Winchell 2013: 14), although the possibility of some of these exotic stones being transported by the streams cannot be completely discarded (Shiner et al. 1971: 392). Nevertheless, the occurrence of Red Sea shells in the tombs at UA 53 may suggest that at least by the end of this period the inhabitants of Eastern Sudan were involved in inter-regional exchange networks. Moreover, the mace heads, which apparently occur only on the largest site, can be regarded as highly meaningful objects, also because of their possible ceremonial use and likely symbolic value (see Shiner et al.1971: 391), well known in the Neolithic contexts of the Nile valley (Salvatori and Usai eds. 2008: 158).

FIGURE 20: LATE BUTANA GROUP GRAVE WITH NINE LIP PLUGS IN EXCAVATION UNIT XVII AT SITE UA 53 (SCALE IN THE IMAGE OF THE LIP PLUGS IN CM).

2.4 A broader perspective on Mesolithic and Neolithic: the emerging complexity

The first results of the resumed fieldwork in Eastern Sudan on the 6th-4th millennia BC phases of the regional sequence fit in a general context characterized by a renewed interest for the study of the Mesolithic and Neolithic periods in the middle Nile valley, and also for a reconsideration of the results of the earlier investigations in the whole region. Regarding the Nile valley in particular, in the Upper Nubian area, for the first time a systematic research project conducted in the last twenty years and focusing on the Early and mid-Holocene allowed to get better insights into the cultural

FIGURE 21: CAWRI SHELL ASSOCIATED WITH SHELL AND OSTRICH EGGSHELL BEADS FROM A LATE BUTANA GROUP GRAVE IN EXCAVATION UNIT XVIII AT SITE UA 53 (SCALE IN CM).

phases preceding the 3rd millennium BC (Honegger 2014a: 19). In that region, fresh evidence was also collected in the field of funerary archaeology, offering a new stimulating perspective on the economy and social organization of the Mesolithic and Neolithic inhabitants of Upper Nubia (Honegger 2014a: 20, 24; Usai and Salvatori eds. 2008: 147-156). In the meantime, in the region of Khartoum, outstanding data suggesting an internal periodisation of the Mesolithic culture of that area were collected for the first time thanks to the systematic adoption of stratigraphic excavation and to the study of the site formation processes and of the post-depositional factors affecting the archaeological sites (Salvatori 2012: 400-402; Usai 2014: 32-35).

As already rightly stressed, in this framework the potential contribution of the ongoing research in Eastern Sudan may add further details to the general understanding of the Sudanese Mesolithic and Neolithic periods, whose complexity is beginning to emerge with the increase of available data, mainly as far as the infra-regional cultural variability is concerned (Salvatori and Usai eds. 2008: 159; Usai 2016: 1). Eastern Sudan in those periods was certainly affected by general environmental processes known at the macro-regional scale. In the meantime, a relationship with the Nile valley, mainly with central Sudan is in the Mesolithic phase shown by the occurrence of the wavy line decoration in Eastern Sudan, as well as by the possibility that the scraped ware itself may have originated in the Nile valley (see above 2.1 *The Pre-Saroba sites and the Amm Adam Group*). Nevertheless, Eastern Sudan confirms to be precociously characterized by regional features evident in the material culture, for the moment mainly shown in the ceramic production by the knobbed ware. Thus, the emerging of a regional tradition is not only marked just by variants of more widely occurring traits, but by a very specific and distinctive feature such as the knobbed ware, distinguishing Eastern Sudan from the Khartoum region and, in general, the Nile valley. Unfortunately, the factors leading to this process remain obscure. Interestingly, different dynamics may have taken place in other areas far from the Nile valley, like the Wadi Howar, where the definition of a regional tradition only occurs in the Late Neolithic phase, starting from *c.* 4000 BC, in connection with the climatic changes leading to drier conditions (Keding 1998: 8-9).

For the moment, the dynamics underlying the indubitable links between the Nile valley and Eastern Sudan shown by the material culture, whose existence was indeed suggested since the very beginning of the exploration of the region (see Marks and Sadr 1988: 72; Shiner *et al.* 1971: 317), remain also unknown. It can be hypothesized that interaction with the Nile valley may have been favored by the seasonal movements made by human groups even in Mesolithic times to exploit periodically available resources, as was suggested for explaining the relationships between Lower Nubia and the Western Desert in the same phase, and for explaining the occurrence of exogenous mineral components in the Mesolithic pottery of the Khartoum region always roughly in the same phase (Usai 2016: 15). Interestingly, this model suggesting a greater mobility certainly complement the traditional view that considers the Mesolithic settlements as basically permanent, and the richness in resources theoretically available in their neighborhood in more humid phases as a factor that limited the seasonal movements of their inhabitants into a range of few kilometers. Actually, while the occurrence of permanent or semi-permanent Mesolithic settlements is certainly supported by the discovery of apparently permanent huts associated with burials at el-Barga, in Upper Nubia (Honegger 2014a: 24), the existence of large permanent Mesolithic villages was recently questioned seriously for the Khartoum region. There only the occurrence of more consistent structures, clearly defined functional areas and garbage pits in some mid-7th millennium BC settlements may be considered with some caution as a marker of a decreased mobility or even sedentism, while a more mobile adaptive system may have been dominant in the early 7th millennium BC, and, also possibly related to the emerging drier climatic conditions, in the 6th millennium BC (Salvatori 2012: 403-404, 412, 434-435; see also Usai 2014: 36, 39, 2016: 14).

In this framework, to explain the above referred similarities of traits of material culture between Eastern Sudan and the Nile valley, it may also be suggested that actual migrations of groups took place from the Nile valley to Eastern Sudan when drier conditions affected central Sudan, whose impact may have been less dramatic in more eastern and southeastern areas closer to the footslopes of the Ethio-Eritrean highlands. Moreover, the possible impact of demographic pressure that may have favored the departure of groups from the regions closer to the Nile valley cannot be excluded.

If the possibility of actual migrations is admitted, it can be expected that the traits shared with the Nile valley would occur in Eastern Sudan only starting in some specific phases, possibly in connection with an increasing number of settlements. Of course, a more thorough investigation on the Mesolithic of Eastern Sudan and the elaboration of a finely tuned periodisation for it are necessary to confirm this model, as well as a better knowledge of the environmental and demographic factors affecting the Mesolithic communities in the Nile valley and neighboring regions. Anyway, it should be remarked that both explanations proposed, i.e. seasonal movements and migrations, does not exclude each other, and possibly both might have taken place. Whatever it is, the recently resumed exploration of the Mesolithic in Eastern Sudan will certainly contribute to the hoped definition of the cultural and social exchanges between the Nile valley and its neighboring regions in those phases (see Salvatori 2012, p. 437).

Actually, this kind of dynamics explaining the relationships between the Nile valley and Eastern Sudan may also have continued in the 5th millennium BC, when productive economy was adopted in the Nile valley of central Sudan, well after Upper Nubia, where livestock breeding was already established in the early 6th millennium BC (Honegger 2014a: 20, 23-24; Salvatori and Usai eds. 2008: 150; Usai 2016: 14) and Near Eastern cultivated cereals occurred at least from the late 6th millennium BC (Usai 2016: 18). In the 5th millennium BC, the less favorable general environmental conditions and the increasing quantitative economic relevance of livestock breeding may have favored seasonal mobility and thus the interaction and exchanges among groups, as also perhaps shown by the study of the body orientation in some cemeteries suggesting their frequentation in specific periods of the year (Salvatori and Usai eds. 2008: 159). Nevertheless, the issue of the degree of mobility and of estimating the real economic relevance of livestock breeding for the Neolithic groups of the Nile valley is far from being solved (see e.g. Honegger 2014a: 28; Salvatori and Usai eds. 2008: 150, 155; Usai 2016: 18). An intense interaction between groups at a regional level is somehow confirmed for Upper Nubia by the homogeneity of anthropological data, of funerary rituals and of ceramic productions (Salvatori and Usai eds. 2008: 158).

In the case of Eastern Sudan, the mobility of at least a part of these groups may not only explain the apparent continuity in the occurrence of stylistic links between the ceramic productions of our region and those of the Nile valley, but may also explain the discovery of shells from the Red Sea in the Neolithic cemeteries in the Nile valley, both in the region of Khartoum and in Upper Nubia (Honegger 2014b: 37; Salvatori and Usai eds. 2008: 72). Moreover, in Upper Nubia too, raw materials from remote regions such as amazonite and obsidian were used to produce personal ornaments found in cemeteries of the region of Kerma (see e.g. Honegger 2014b: 35). Particularly, it is highly possible that the Red Sea shells found at the Neolithic archaeological sites in the Nile valley of central Sudan were actually brought there via the Eastern Sudan and the Butana, while the obsidian from Upper Nubian cemeteries may have arrived from the obsidian sources in the Danakil depression via the Eastern Sudan and perhaps the Eastern Desert.

Through those interactions with the Nile valley, domesticated livestock may have also reached Eastern Sudan and may have adapted to life there. Perhaps the interactions with central Sudan were favored by the same drier climatic conditions characterizing the mid-Holocene and stimulating the emergence of a food producing economy in the Western Sahara and in the Nile valley (see Close 2002; Hassan 2002: 12-16), and later on the spread of a productive economy towards the central Sudan, perhaps also related to the movements of human groups (Usai 2016: 19). Although it can be debated if the domesticated animal species arrived to Nubia and to the Sudan from the Sahara or via the Egyptian Nile valley (Honegger

2014a: 27; Usai 2016: 17), in Eastern Sudan, domesticated bovines very likely arrived from the middle Nile, and the same can be quite safely imagined for the caprovines. Nevertheless, despite its role in that process remains largely underestimated, the Eastern Desert may have been a further corridor for the diffusion of domestic livestock towards Eastern Sudan, as the very precocious -but so far unfortunately isolated- occurrence of domesticated caprovines at Sodmein cave may suggest (Vermeersch *et al.* 2015: 483-489).

The occurrence of domesticated livestock, both bovines and caprovines, is of course evident in the archaeological records of Eastern Sudan only from the 4th millennium BC, when domesticated barley also occurs in the Butana Group assemblages (see above 2. 3 *The Butana Group*). We may wonder if this later adoption compared with the Nile valley is just a matter of gaps in the archaeological investigation of Eastern Sudan, especially as far as the Malawiya Group is concerned (see also Shiner *et al.* 1971: 328), and if the process of adoption of domesticated animals and plants in our region may have started even earlier than the 4th millennium BC. Nevertheless, the late adoption of a productive economy in Eastern Sudan may be justified by the more humid environment lasting longer in the regions close to the Ethio-Eritrean highlands. Interestingly, this last hypothesis also seems to be in agreement with the general macro-regional framework, characterized by the adoption of domesticated livestock on the Ethio-Eritrean highlands only in the early 2nd millennium BC, i.e. c. 3000 years later than in the Nile valley of central Sudan (Lesur *et al.* 2008: 152-153). Actually, the first occurrence of domesticated livestock in Eastern Sudan in the 4th millennium BC seems to fit well with the location of the region between the Nile valley and the Ethio-Eritrean highlands, and may indirectly confirm that Eastern Sudan may have played a role in the process of diffusing domesticated animals and plants towards the Ethio-Eritrean highlands, or at least towards their northwestern slopes (Lesur *et al.* 2008: 153-154).

In the same phase, the adoption of the domesticated crops originating from the Near East via the Nile valley may also have had an impact in the strategies of the exploitation of local vegetal species such as sorghum, that ultimately demonstrated to be much more suitable to the general local environmental conditions than the Near Eastern crops. This may be the starting point of a process that may have led to the emergence of morphologically domesticated sorghum at least in the early 2nd millennium BC. This process may have taken the whole time period of the Butana Group, when an agro-pastoral economy was certainly adopted in Eastern Sudan (see above 2. 3 The Butana Group). If at the very beginning the newly adopted domesticated animals and crops may have been marginal in terms of economic importance, as shown e.g. by the above described intense exploitation of land snails in early Butana Group times, by the end of the 4th-early 3rd millennium BC they may have been crucial, as suggested by the overwhelming frequency of domesticated livestock at the end of the Butana Group phase (see above 2. 3 *The Butana Group*). It can also be suggested that a crucial factor in the emergence of the larger and apparently more permanent settlements characterizing the Butana Group was represented by the widespread adoption of domesticated animals and by the cultivation of Near Eastern and Sahelian vegetal species, although the latter apparently not yet morphologically domesticated.

Even if the evidence available for the Butana Group is on the whole very limited, this phase may have seen the emergence of social hierarchy in Eastern Sudan, as suggested by the occurrence of exotic grave goods such as Red Sea shells in some tombs, and by the occurrence of objects to be regarded as possible symbols of authority and rank markers such as the mace heads (see above 2. 3 *The Butana Group*). Similar processes are also known in the Nile valley, where they are evident and perhaps started from the early 6th millennium BC and were very likely rooted on the possibility of control of resources such as domestic livestock (Honegger 2004: 30; Salvatori and Usai eds. 2008: 152, 158; Usai 2016: 17). In particular, the circulation of exotic and luxury objects, in which Eastern Sudan was rich (see 1.4 *The resources*), may have been increasing because those objects often became rank markers. The rise of highly articulated hierarchic societies in Egypt, Lower and Upper Nubia may have favored the establishment of long distance networks along which luxury materials were circulated (Wengrow 2006: 138-140, 166-167), perhaps already involving Eastern Sudan and somehow prefiguring a pattern well known for the later phases (see below 3.3 *Between Kush and Egypt*). As far as the relations with Upper Nubia that all this may have favored, an indirect confirmation of their presence may be represented by the above mentioned similarities between the Butana Group ceramics and the Pre-Kerma ones (see above 2. 3 *The Butana Group*).

Chapter 3
In a fledging network (c. 3000-1000 BC)

3.1 The Gash Group

Deeply related to the Butana Group, this culture is the better known component of the cultural sequence of Eastern Sudan, because one of the largest Gash Group sites, Mahal Teglinos (K 1), near the modern city of Kassala, was investigated from 1980 to 1995 (Fattovich 1989b, 1991a: 105-108, 1993a; Fattovich, Manzo and Usai 1994) and more recently in 2010, and from 2013 onwards (Manzo et al. 2011: 27-30; Manzo 2014a: 376-379, 2015: 231-233, 2016: 191-194). Moreover, in addition to the ones where surface collections were made in the Eighties, other Gash Group sites were surveyed in 2010 and 2011 (Manzo et al. 2012: 117-123).

The chronology of the Gash Group is based on twelve radiocarbon dates from Mahal Teglinos (K 1):[6] they suggest a date between the mid-3rd and the first part of the 2nd millennia BC for this culture. Although it was thought that the duration of the Gash Group could extend up to the mid-2nd millennium BC, and that the bad preservation of the upper layers at Mahal Teglinos (K 1) could have prevented the collection of organic remains suitable for radiocarbon dating from assemblages of the last phases of the Gash Group, a recently investigated stratigraphic sequence clearly showed that the transition to the following phase took place around 1800 BC (Manzo nd.a).

A general sequence for the Gash Group ceramics from Mahal Teglinos (K 1) was outlined, and four different phases were distinguished (Capuano, Manzo and Perlingieri 1994: 114; Fattovich 1989b: 223, 229-231, 1990a: 16-17, 1991a: 104, 1993a: 246-248, 1993b: 439-441; Fattovich, Sadr and Vitagliano 1988-1989: 332-333; see also Fattovich 1989a: 490; Manzo 2014a: 379, 2015: 232-233; Sadr 1991: 41). The Early Gash Group phase, dating around the mid 3rd millennium BC, was characterized by bowls decorated with comb impressed bands often extending to the body of the vessel, rim bands obtained with impressions of a punch (Figure 22 a) or with rocker movement of a double teethed tool, plain bowls with notches on top of the lip (Figure 22 b), accurately scraped and wiped ware, and a distinctive vegetal tempered ware; the Middle Gash Group phase, dating to the last centuries of the 3rd millennium BC, was characterized by accurate black cups with regular rim bands forming rail track patterns and gray black greasy slip (Figure 22 c-d); the Classic Gash Group phase, dating to the end of the 3rd–very beginning of the 2nd millennium BC, was characterized by bowls and cups often distinguished by flat lips and decorated with accurately impressed rim bands and sometimes red slip on the top of the lip (Figure 22 e); the Late Gash Group phase, dating to the beginning of the 2nd millennium BC, was mainly characterized by bowls and cups decorated with impressed or incised rim bands, patterns of crossed lines forming rim bands, decoration consisting of parallel horizontal grooves sometimes crossed by oblique grooves (Figure 22 f), finger nail ware, abundant scraped ware sometimes with modeled clay decoration, and often with pinched and indented rims (Figure 22 g-h).

Exotic ceramics showing similarities with Kerma, C-Group, Pan-Grave and Yemeni Bronze age types (Figure 23) were collected at Mahal Teglinos (K 1) in assemblages related to the different phases of the Gash Group culture. At least in some cases they may well have been imports, while in other cases a local production seems likely (Fattovich 1989b: 252-253, 1990a: 15, 17-18, 1991a: 107-108, 1991b,

---

[6] Fattovich 1993 a, 230, 246, unspecified laboratory: 3860±60 bp; Gif 7651: 3780±90 bp; Gif 7652: 4010±90 bp; Gif 7653: 3980±90 bp. Manzo et al. 2012, 128, Beta 311299: 3740±30 bp; Manzo nd.a, Beta 401122: 3570±30 bp; Alemseged Beldados et al. nd.a, Beta 380246: 3560±30 bp; unpublished dates, Beta 404210: 3770±30 bp; Beta 428646: 4140±30 bp; Beta 437215: 3740±30 bp; Beta 437216: 3380±30; Beta 437217: 3750±30 bp.

Figure 22: fragments of Gash Group ceramics from site Mahal Teglinos (K 1): a) rim of a cup decorated with a band of punch impressions from an Early Gash Group assemblage in excavation unit XII; b) rim of a bowl with impressions on the lip from an Early Gash Group assemblage in excavation unit XII; c) rim of a cup with rail track regular rim band and light scraping outside from a Middle Gash Group assemblage in excavation unit X; d) rim of a dish with regular impressed banded decoration and black greasy slip from a Middle Gash Group assemblage in excavation unit X; e) rim of a bowl with flat lip and decorated with accurately impressed rim band from a Classic Gash Group assemblage in excavation unit VII; f) rim of a bowl with a band of wide and shallow horizontal parallel grooves from a Late Gash Group assemblage in excavation unit IX; g-h) rims of scraped ware bowls respectively with pinched and impressed decoration on the lip from Late Gash Group assemblages in excavation unit IX (scale in cm).

1993b: 443-444; Manzo 1997, 2012: 77-78, 2014b: 1150-1152; Manzo *et al.* 2012: 60). Interestingly, a vessel of Kerma ancien I/C-Group Ib type was found in a badly eroded double tomb containing two skeletons with contracted legs in the western Gash Group cemetery at Mahal Teglinos (K 1) (Figure 24): this is very different from the other tombs in that cemetery -usually single and with skeletons in extended position- and may even suggest the presence of Nubians at the site or alternatively the adoption of a Nubian -most likely Kerma- funerary ritual by local people (Manzo 2016: 193).

Figure 23: sherds of Yemeni Bronze age type from Gash Group assemblages in excavation unit BSKP-Q at site Mahal Teglinos (K 1) (scale in cm).

Of course, all this suggests the involvement of the region in a broad network of long-range contacts, also confirmed by the fact that some Gash Group personal ornaments were made from Red Sea shells and sometimes also included imported *faïence* beads (see below) (Figure 25). Moreover, the fact that the largest collection of Egyptian ceramic materials south of Upper Nubia, including materials dating at least from the First Intermediate Period to the end of the Middle Kingdom was found at Mahal Teglinos (K 1) in Gash Groups assemblages certainly supports this hypothesis (Manzo 1993, 1997: 79, 2012: 77, 2014a: 378, 2015: 233, 2016: 192, nd.b) (Figure 26). Interestingly, the Egyptian materials from Mahal Teglinos in certain cases are quite unusual if compared with the ones from contemporary Upper Nubian contexts. On the other hand, sherds from Eastern Sudan were found in some Eastern Desert sites (Manzo 2012: 81-82), scattered sherds and vessels reminiscent of Gash Group types from the Eastern Sudan were recorded in some sites on the Fourth Cataract, as shown e.g. by a pot with finger nail impressions from a Kerma moyen tomb excavated in that area (Paner 2014: Pl. 21, middle column, upper row), and even in Egypt, on the Red Sea coast, at Mersa/Wadi Gawasis, the Middle Kingdom harbor to the land of Punt (Manzo 2012: 76).

Interestingly, the culture of the Gash Group was not limited to the region between Atbara and Gash and to the Gash delta: it certainly extended to the region of Agordat in the Eritrean western lowlands (Brandt *et al.* 2008: 43-44; see also Fattovich 1989a: 494, 1993b: 439), perhaps to the southern fringes of the Eastern Desert, as was suggested on the basis of finds from Erkowit (Waida and Kabir 2003: 64-65; see also Fattovich 1993b: 439), and maintained relationships with the sites of the Butana, as perhaps shown by parallelism with finds from Shaqadud, like e.g. in the case of the finger nail pottery (Fattovich 1990a: 18, 1991b:

Figure 24: Kerma ancien I-C-Group Ib vessel found in a badly eroded double tomb in the western cemetery of site Mahal Teglinos (K 1) (excavation unit XII; scale in cm).

Figure 25: A Gash Group tomb in the western cemetery at site Mahal Teglinos (K 1) (excavation unit BPLF-Z/BPQA-E) characterized by a *faïence* beads bracelet and a cawri shells anklet.

45).

The Gash Group lithic industry is characterized in the earliest phases by multiple platform cores, flakes from multiple platform cores, blades from opposite platform cores, the prevailing tools are perforators and the prevailing raw material is agate, while in the last phase the opposite platform cores are very typical, together with flakes from single platform cores, blades from single and multiple platform cores, backed pieces, and quartz is the prevailing raw material with a peak in the use of flint and the worthy occurrence of few scattered flakes of obsidian possibly imported from sources in Ethiopia or Eritrea (Fattovich 1990a: 18, 1993b: 440; Usai 1997: 94-95, 2002: 187, 189-190; Manzo 2015: 232). The number of grinding stones from Gash Group sites may suggest that plant exploitation was crucial in the economy of this culture (Fattovich 1993b: 440; Marks and Sadr 1988: 79).

At Mahal Teglinos (K 1) sealings (Figure 27 a) and administrative devices such as tokens and mushroom shaped objects also found at Kerma and regarded as seals were

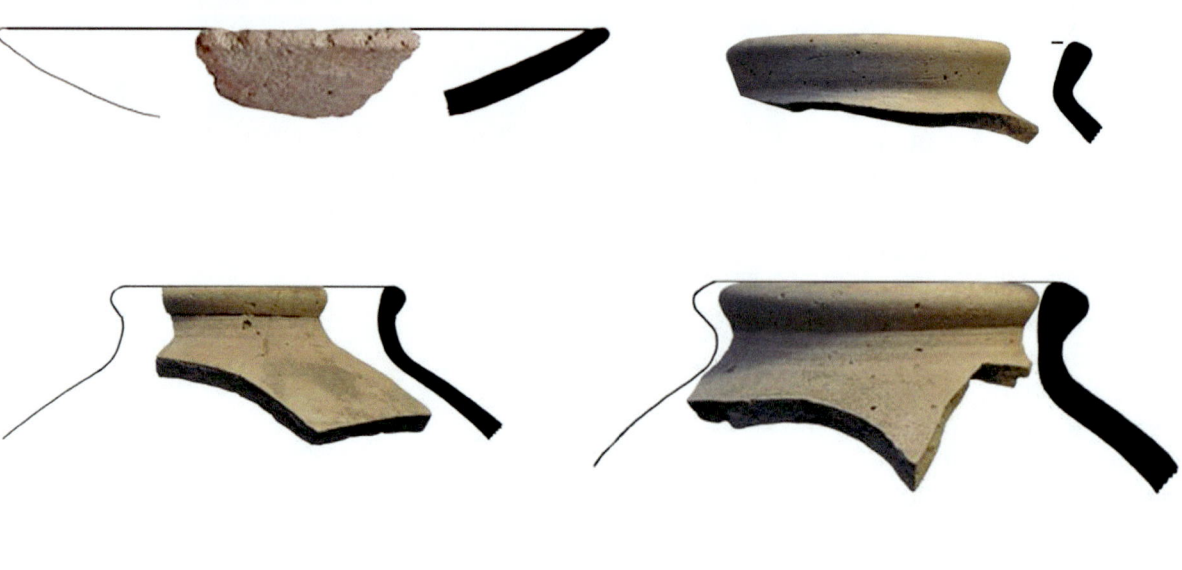

Figure 26: rim sherds of late First Intermediate Period – early Middle Kingdom Egyptian jars and dish from a Gash Group assemblage in excavation unit X at site Mahal Teglinos (K 1) (scale in cm).

Figure 27: ADMINISTRATIVE DEVICES FROM SITE MAHAL TEGLINOS (K 1): A) SEALING FROM A MIDDLE GASH GROUP ASSEMBLAGE IN EXCAVATION UNIT X; B) MUSHROOM SHAPED OBJECT, POSSIBLY A SEAL, FROM A LATE GASH GROUP ASSEMBLAGE IN EXCAVATION UNIT VI (SCALE IN CM).

found (Fattovich 1991a: 108, 1991c: 72-73, 1993b: 444, 1995: 193-194; Manzo 2007: 51-54, 2015: 232-233) (Figure 27 b). This may suggest that there was an organized management of some commodities, and that the administrative techniques may have been somehow related to those of Upper Nubia.

As far as the subsistence economy of this phase is concerned, both remains of wild and domesticated plants have been collected: among them the occurrence of wild and domesticated sorghum, the earliest so far recorded in Africa, and of rare remains of millet, barley and wheat, and of baobab grains from the western Sahel should be stressed (Alemseged Beldados 2015: 79-80, Table 8.2; Costantini *et al.* 1982: 33; Manzo 2014a: 384-385; Alemseged Beldados *et al.* nd.a) (Table 1). Also, the zoological remains are characterized by the co-presence of wild and domesticated species such as freshwater gasteropods, fish, reptiles, birds, mammalian game and livestock, which is dominant with an apparently increasing importance of cattle (Gautier and Van Neer 2006: 231-232; Geraads 1983) (Tables 2-4).

The Gash Group sites occur mostly across the area of Shurab el-Gash and close to the Gash river, in the northwestern end of the Gash delta, near Eriba Station, while some are also located between the Gash and the Atbara, usually near the modern cultivated areas or close to little streams (Fattovich 1989a: 492, 1990a: 17, 1991a: 99-104, 1993b: 439, 442; Manzo *et al.* 2012: 44; Marks and Fattovich 1989: 455; Sadr 1988: 392, 395, 1991: 41) (Figures 28-29). The thickness of the deposit of some of them and their dimensions suggest a permanent or at least recurrent occupation for the major sites such as Mahal Teglinos (K 1) and perhaps Jebel Abu Gamal (JAG) 1. The structured and articulated settlement pattern of the Gash Group was regarded as a possible evidence of social hierarchy (see Fattovich 1995: 192; Fattovich, Sadr and Vitagliano 1988-1989: 339-340, Sadr 1991: 65-66). Interestingly, the location of Mahal Teglinos (K 1) seems somehow eccentric and isolated in the context of the Gash Group settlement pattern (Fattovich 1995: 192; Fattovich, Sadr and Vitagliano 1988-1989: 338). In general, both the distribution of the sites through the region and the presence of permanent or semi-permanent sites seem in agreement with an agro-pastoral economy suggested for this culture by the archaeozoological and palaeobotanical studies.

As far as the organization of the largest Gash Group site so far known, Mahal Teglinos (K 1), which extends for more than 10 hectares, is concerned, two large cemeteries intensively used from the 3rd to the early 2nd millennia BC are located in the eastern and western sectors of the site, with a settlement area in the middle dating to the same phases, while a further settlement area developed on the westernmost fringes of the site at the end of the Gash Group, in a sector previously occupied by a small lake (Figure 30).

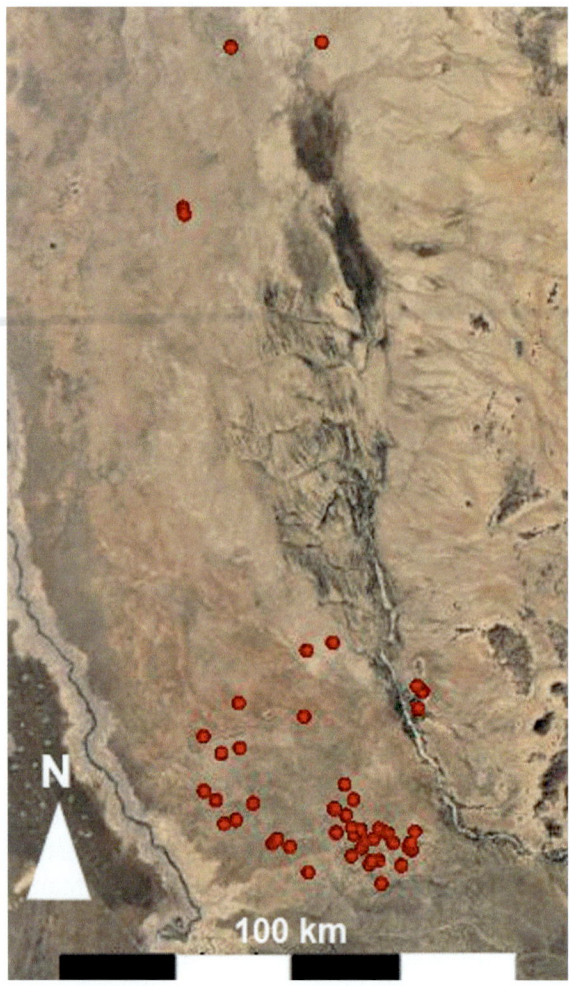

FIGURE 28: MAP SHOWING THE DISTRIBUTION OF THE GASH GROUP SITES BETWEEN THE ATBARA AND THE GASH RIVERS AND THE IN THE GASH DELTA (PLOTTED ON GOOGLE EARTH SATELLITE IMAGE).

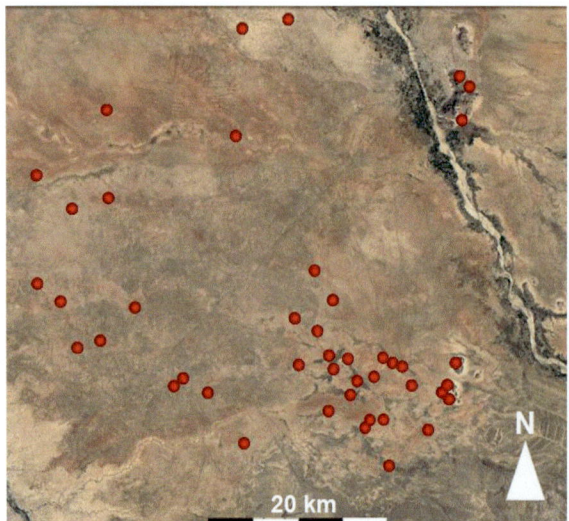

FIGURE 29: DETAIL SHOWING THE DISTRIBUTION OF THE GASH GROUP SITES BETWEEN THE ATBARA AND THE GASH RIVERS (PLOTTED ON GOOGLE EARTH SATELLITE IMAGE).

Different kinds of structures are associated with the Gash Group settlement area in the central sector of Mahal Teglinos (K 1). Traces of light rounded huts whose perimeters were marked by hard clay soil in association with stone structures too, possibly the remains of bases for domestic facilities, were brought to light, and go back to the early 2nd millennium BC on pottery evidence (Fattovich, Manzo and Usai 1994: 14-15). Earlier remains of a settlement with huts are represented by post holes dating to the late 3rd millennium BC on the eastern fringes of the central sector of the site (Fattovich, Manzo and Usai 1994: 15). At Mahal Teglinos (K 1), remains of mud and also mud brick structures, dating from the 3rd to the early 2nd millennium BC were found. They represent the southernmost examples of mud and mud bricks structures in Africa in the 3rd and 2nd millennia BC, and as a matter of fact the only ones south of Upper Nubia in that period. The earliest structure, going back to 3rd millennium BC, was recorded on the eastern fringes of the central sector of the site: it was also characterized by associated fireplaces and, after the end of its use, was overlapped by the eastern cemetery, as sometimes happens on the edge of the cemeteries bordering the settlement area (Fattovich 1995: 197; Fattovich, Manzo and Usai 1994: 15). A better preserved mud brick structure with a couple of small rectangular rooms and a larger elongated one was investigated in the central sector of the site and goes back to the early 2nd millennium BC (Fattovich 1995: 197; Fattovich, Manzo and Usai 1994: 16) (Figure 31).

In the central sector of the site a large area used for the preparation and consumption of food dating to the last part of the 3rd millennium BC was discovered, and may have been related to the preparation of ceremonial meals, as suggested by its location between the two cemeteries, and by the intense use and scale of the activities that took place there (Manzo 2015: 232-233, 2016: 192). Interestingly, after the use, vessels and other artifacts like administrative devices were carefully deposited inside the firepits. Among them, it is worth noting the occurrence of large rounded trays reminiscent of the ethnographic *dokka*, often found collapsed into the firepits: they may have been used to prepare sorghum bread (Figure 32). Also in the same area, a concentration of imported First Intermediate Period-early Middle Kingdom Egyptian sherds (see also Manzo nd.b) and small clay statuettes of lions so far unique in the region were collected.

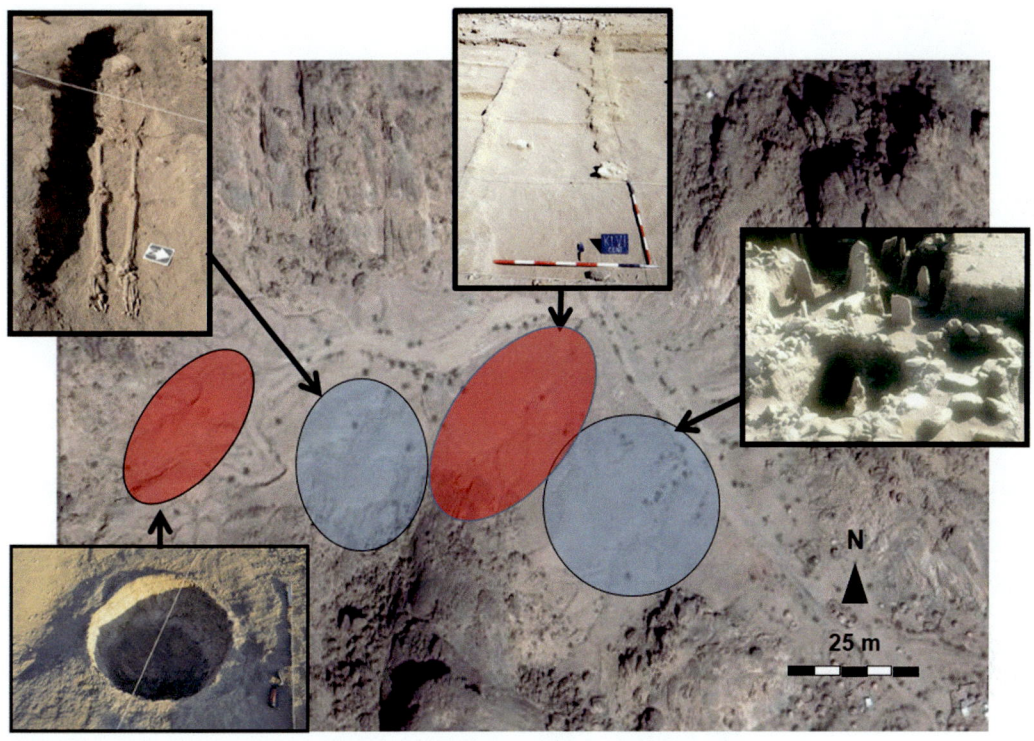

Figure 30: functional areas at Mahal Teglinos (K 1) in Gash Group times, the red highlight shows the settlement areas, the blue one the cemeteries, details of some structures in the different sectors are also shown.

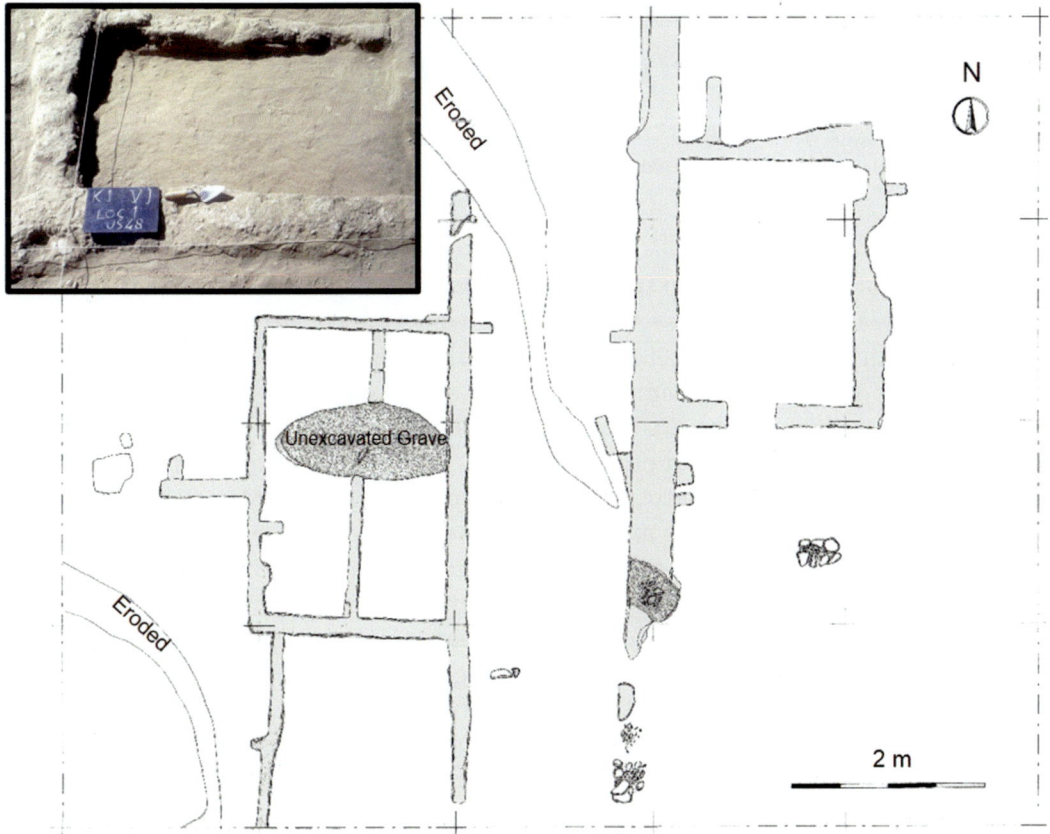

Figure 31: early 2nd millennium BC mud brick structure in excavation unit BSQV-Y/BVAA-T in the central sector of the site Mahal Teglinos (K 1), plan and detail.

Figure 32: fragments of a large rounded tray in a fireplace of the Middle Gash Group food preparation area in excavation unit X in the central sector of the site Mahal Teglinos (K 1), and reconstruction of its diameter (scale in the image showing the reconstruction in cm).

Noteworthy, a part of the Gash Group settlement at the very beginning of the 2nd millennium BC extended over an area in the western sector of the site which may have been previously occupied by a small lake, which dried up around 2000 BC, possibly showing the local impact of drier conditions affecting the whole region, in agreement with the above outlined general climatic trends of northeastern Africa (see paragraph 2.1 *Present and past environment*). In this sector of the site, the late Gash Group settlement consisted of rounded huts whose perimeter is outlined by post holes also associated with storage pits (Fattovich, Manzo and Usai 1994: 17; Manzo 2015: 233). It should be remarked that always in the same area previously occupied by the now dried lake, a shallow pit was possibly used for rubbish disposal at the very end of the Gash Group, and gave very useful information on the economy and way of life of the inhabitants of the site in that period (Manzo 2014a: 378, 2015: 232). Among the finds, big pieces of a large clay storage container, perhaps similar to the Nubian ethnographic *gusseba* used for the storage of grains, whose fabric was characterized by vegetal inclusions, were collected in this spot. Moreover, it should be remarked that the need itself of finding a solution for the disposal rubbish, strongly supports the hypothesis that this specific Gash Group site was permanently settled at that time (see Hardy-Smith and Edwards 2004). In this area a further typology of Gash Group oven was recorded: it consisted of a very regular rounded pit with whitened burned stones perhaps used as baking stones at the bottom (Manzo 2014a: 378).

The eastern cemetery at Mahal Teglinos was characterized by a very intense use from at least the mid-3rd to the early 2nd millennia BC. In this sector, different attitudes of body deposition occur: extended on the back sometimes with a flexed arm at a right angle, slightly flexed, and, in the earliest phase of use, fully flexed legs and even contracted position, all with a highly variable orientation (Fattovich 1991a: 105-107, 1993a: 238, 241-242, 253, 1993b: 440-441, 1995: 294-196; Fattovich, Manzo and Usai 1994: 15; see also Fattovich 1990b: 19). No grave goods were collected except for personal ornaments (Fattovich 1993a: 238, 241-242, 253). Interestingly, the bodies in contracted or flexed position of the earliest phase of use were sometimes associated with red ochre, possibly originally applied to a leather cover (Fattovich, Manzo and Usai 1994: 15-16) (Figure 33), a trait similar to that of the Kerma graves of the Fourth Cataract region (Paner 2014: 55-56, 63, 65). For several graves no superstructure was remarked, perhaps

Figure 33: Early Gash Group grave containing a body with contracted legs and remains of red ochre in the eastern cemetery of the site at Mahal Teglinos (K 1) (excavation unit BSPE-J/BSQA-F and BSQK).

Figure 34: Gash Group funerary stelae in the eastern cemetery of the site Mahal Teglinos (K 1).

due to the intense funerary use of the area (Fattovich 1993a: 240, 260), but several small un-inscribed granite stelae, flat, quadrangular in section or pointed in shape and 70 to 110cm in height, were erected on successive floor surfaces from where some pits were cut and are sometimes associated with concentrations of animal bones, suggesting that funerary offerings may have taken place there (Fattovich 1989c: 56-58, 1991a: 105, 1993a: 236, 240, 1995: 196-197) (Figure 34). A possible later ceremonial and funerary use of the area, always dating to Gash Group times may be represented by some stone cairns sometimes associated with heads of bovines and some burials (Fattovich 1989b: 231, 1990b: 20, 1993a: 237-239).

An intense and repeated funerary use dating from c. 2700 to c. 2000 BC was also remarked in the western cemetery, where fireplaces and concentrations of fragmented vessels and animal bones associated with stelae and structures made of stone slabs perhaps related to ritual funerary offerings were remarked as well (Fattovich, Manzo and Usai 1994: 16-17; Manzo 2016: 193). In this cemetery, a greater uniformity of the position of the skeletons was remarked, as the great majority is in extended position on the back with some examples on the side, but like in the eastern cemetery, in some cases the right angle flexed arm was remarked and the orientation remains highly variable (Fattovich, Manzo and Usai 1994: 16; Manzo 2016: 192-194). Interestingly, some of the tombs in the western cemetery contained two bodies and it was suggested that one of the two may represent a sacrificed person (Manzo 2014c: 16, Fig. 7, 2016: 193) (Figure 35). As previously remarked, a specific double grave, where the bodies were also characterized by the fact that their legs were in contracted position was found in association with a Kerma ancien I/C-Group Ib vessel (see above). Moreover, in addition to the usual personal ornaments, sometimes made from Red Sea shells, eleven tombs investigated in this cemetery were also characterized by grave goods represented by locally made vessels (Fattovich, Manzo and Usai 1994: 17; Manzo 2012: 77, 2014b, 1152; Manzo et al. 2012: 96-97) (Figure 36 a-b). Also noteworthy is the occurrence of imported *faïence* beads among the grave goods (Manzo 2012: 77) (see above). A systematic anthropological study of the human remains is in progress but unfortunately this was possible only for the tombs excavated in the last field seasons in the western cemetery and for the few samples exported to Italy in the Eighties, as the other remains from the older excavations were lost in a recent flood of the Gash river that destroyed the storeroom of the expedition.

FIGURE 35: MIDDLE GASH GROUP GRAVE IN THE WESTERN CEMETERY OF THE SITE MAHAL TEGLINOS (K 1) (EXCAVATION UNIT XII), IT CONTAINS THE MAIN BURIAL WITH THE BODY IN EXTENDED POSITION AND CAWRI BRACELET AS WELL AS A POSSIBLE SACRIFICED INDIVIDUAL IN HIGHLY CONTRACTED POSITION IMMEDIATELY UNDERNEATH THE LEFT LEG OF THE MAIN BURIAL (SCALE IN THE DETAIL SHOWING THE BRACELET IN CM).

Figure 36: complete vessels from the western cemetery (excavation unit XII) of the site Mahal Teglinos (K 1): a) bowl with impressed decoration from an Early Gash Group grave; b) scraped ware jar from a Middle Gash Group grave (scale in cm).

3.2 The Jebel Mokram Group

This culture was described on the basis of surface collections from sites in the region between the Gash and the Atbara and closer to the Gash river, as well as on the basis of assemblages from test pits and limited excavations conducted at some of these sites such as N 100, N 120, Mahal Teglinos (K 1), and in the last years UA 53 (Fattovich 1989b: 233, 1993a: 230-231; Fattovich, Manzo and Usai 1994: 17; Marks and Fattovich 1989: 457; Manzo et al. 2011: 27-30; Manzo et al. 2012: 6-21; Manzo 2015: 232; Shiner et al. 1971: 396-412).

The absolute chronology of this culture is based on five radiocarbon dates ranging from the early 2nd millennium BC to the late 2nd-early 1st millennium BC.[7] Evidence from Mahal Teglinos (K 1) suggests a quick transition between the Gash Group and the Jebel Mokram Group around ca. 1800 BC (Manzo nd.a).

The pottery, whose similarities with the Kerma, C-Group and, especially, Pan-Grave materials have been widely remarked, is characterized by thick and rounded rims, often separated from the body by a groove or a deep incision, vessels whose upper part is covered by crossing incisions forming a regular net pattern (Figure 37 a), or by more spaced crossing parallel lines (Fig. 37 b) often in association with black topped vessels (Fig. 37 c), by vessels completely covered by rocker impressions sometimes crossed by incised lines (Figure 37 d) or by horizontal or vertical parallel grooves (Figure 37 e), while the scraped ware and the rim bands (Figure 37 f) already occurring in the Gash Group, although less frequent, are always present, showing a certain degree of continuity with the previous phase (Fattovich 1989a: 495-496, 1989b: 233, Fig. 8, 1990a: 19, 1991a: 109, Fig. 9-10; Fattovich, Marks and Mohammed Ali 1984: 182, Fig. 6; Manzo et al. 2011: 28-29, 2012: 60-65; Marks and Fattovich 1989: 456; Sadr 1987: 272-276, Fig. 5,

---

[7] Shiner et al. 1971, p. 398 TX 446: 3050±90 bp ; Manzo nd.a Beta-401120: 3440±30; Beta-401121: 3270±30; Beta-404209: 3530±30; Beta-404212: 3450±30.

Figure 37: fragments of Jebel Mokram Group ceramics from excavation unit VI at the site Mahal Teglinos (K 1): a) rim fragment of a bowl with the upper part covered by incised net pattern; b) rim fragment of a bowl with the upper part covered by incised crossing parallel lines; c) rim fragment of a black topped bowl with the upper part covered by crossing incised parallel lines; d) fragment of a black topped vessel completely covered by rocker impressions crossed by incised lines; e) rim fragment of a bowl covered by vertical parallel grooves; f) fragment of the rim of a rim banded bowl (scale in cm).

1990: 69-70, Fig. 5, p-z', 1991, p. 45; Shiner *et al.* 1971: 400-402, Fig. 24, Fig. 25 a-b, 409-410). It should be pointed out that most of the ceramic types characterizing the Jebel Mokram Group assemblages, date in Upper Egypt and Nubia to the first half of the 2nd millennium BC (Sadr 1987: 283), while it was previously thought that they would have appeared in Eastern Sudan only around 1500 BC (Sadr 1991: 106-108; Weschenfelder 2014: 359). The fact that these element appeared roughly at the same time in Eastern Sudan and in the Egyptian and Nubian Nile valley is also confirmed by new comparisons that can now be established with the materials from the Fourth Cataract area recovered in recent years and seems to be coherent with the new chronology suggested by the radiocarbon dates recently obtained for the earliest Jebel Mokram Group assemblages at Mahal Teglinos (K 1) (Manzo 2012: 77-78; Manzo *et al.* 2011: 29-30, 2012: 64; Manzo nd.a). Interestingly, these types may have survived in Eastern Sudan up to the late 2nd-early 1st millennium BC, as suggested by the fact that in presumably later Jebel Mokram Group assemblages they are associated with fragments reminiscent of the Ethiopian pre-Aksumite types (Manzo *et al.* 2012: 65; Manzo nd.a).

Also the Jebel Mokram Group like the Gash Group may not have been limited to the region between the Gash and the Atbara: Jebel Mokram Group materials were collected at Agordat, in the western Eritrean lowlands (Brandt *et al.* 2008: 44) and possibly at Erkowit in the Red Sea hills (Waida and Kabir 2003: 65).

Figure 38: imported ceramic materials from Jebel Mokram Group assemblages: a) fragment of a C-Group II b vessel from excavation unit IX at site UA 53; b) fragment of an Upper Egyptian Marl A4 vessel from excavation unit IX at site UA 53 (scale in cm).

At site UA 53, Jebel Mokram Group assemblages gave fragments of a C-Group II b vessel (Figure 38 a) and of an Upper Egyptian Marl A4 vessel (Manzo *et al.* 2012: 64-65; Manzo nd.b) (Figure 38 b), while a further Egyptian fragment was also found in a Jebel Mokram Group assemblage at Mahal Teglinos (K 1) (Manzo nd.b). Interestingly, the shape of stone axes found in association with Jebel Mokram Group materials has been compared with the one of Kerma stone axes and in some specific cases, more convincingly, to Egyptian early New Kingdom metal specimens (Manzo 2012: 78; Manzo nd.a see also Sadr 1987: 283) (Figure 39). All these finds not only seem to support the above proposed chronology, but also seem to suggest that, like the Gash Group, the Jebel Mokram Group continued to be somehow involved in long-distance exchanges (see also Sadr 1990: 79-80).

A possible seal collected at site JAG 1 and possibly from a Jebel Mokram Group assemblage may suggest that also in this phase a kind of administration and control on the circulation of commodities may have existed (Fattovich 1991c: 69). Interestingly, its flat oval shape is different from the one of the earlier Gash Group mushroom shaped seals and reminiscent of some Kerma Upper Nubian scaraboids (see Reisner 1923: Pl. 40, 1) (Figure 40).

Figure 39: stone axe whose shape is similar to Egyptian early New Kingdom metal specimens from a Jebel Mokram Group assemblage at site UA 53 (scale in cm).

Figure 40: flat oval shaped seal possibly from a Jebel Mokram Group assemblage at site JAG 1 (scale in cm).

The Jebel Mokram Group lithics are characterized by opposite platform cores, while flakes from single platform cores, notches, denticulates and geometrics are the dominating tools; quartz is the preferred raw material (Shiner *et al.* 1971: pp. 399-400, 406-407, Fig. 26; Usai 1997: 94). Interestingly, the occurrence of obsidian in Jebel Mokram Group lithic assemblages, already remarked in the first phases of the archaeological exploration of the region (Fattovich, Marks and Mohammed Ali 1984: 185), was recently confirmed by finds from reliable assemblages at Mahal Teglinos (K 1). As in the case of the obsidian from Gash Group assemblages, this may have been imported from obsidian sources in Eritrea or Ethiopia. Moreover, grinding stones also occur in the Jebel Mokram Group assemblages (Shiner *et al.* 1971: 412, 419).

Excavations at UA 53 gave interesting insights into the domestic architecture of the Jebel Mokram Group, considerably enriching what was known from the previous investigations. Remains of a large circular hut or fence delimited by the holes where the posts were fixed and of more elongated huts with a rounded perimeter were discovered there (Manzo *et al.* 2012: 13-14, 21) (Figure 41). The use of earthen architecture in Jebel Mokram Group times, although perfectly plausible also in light of the evidence

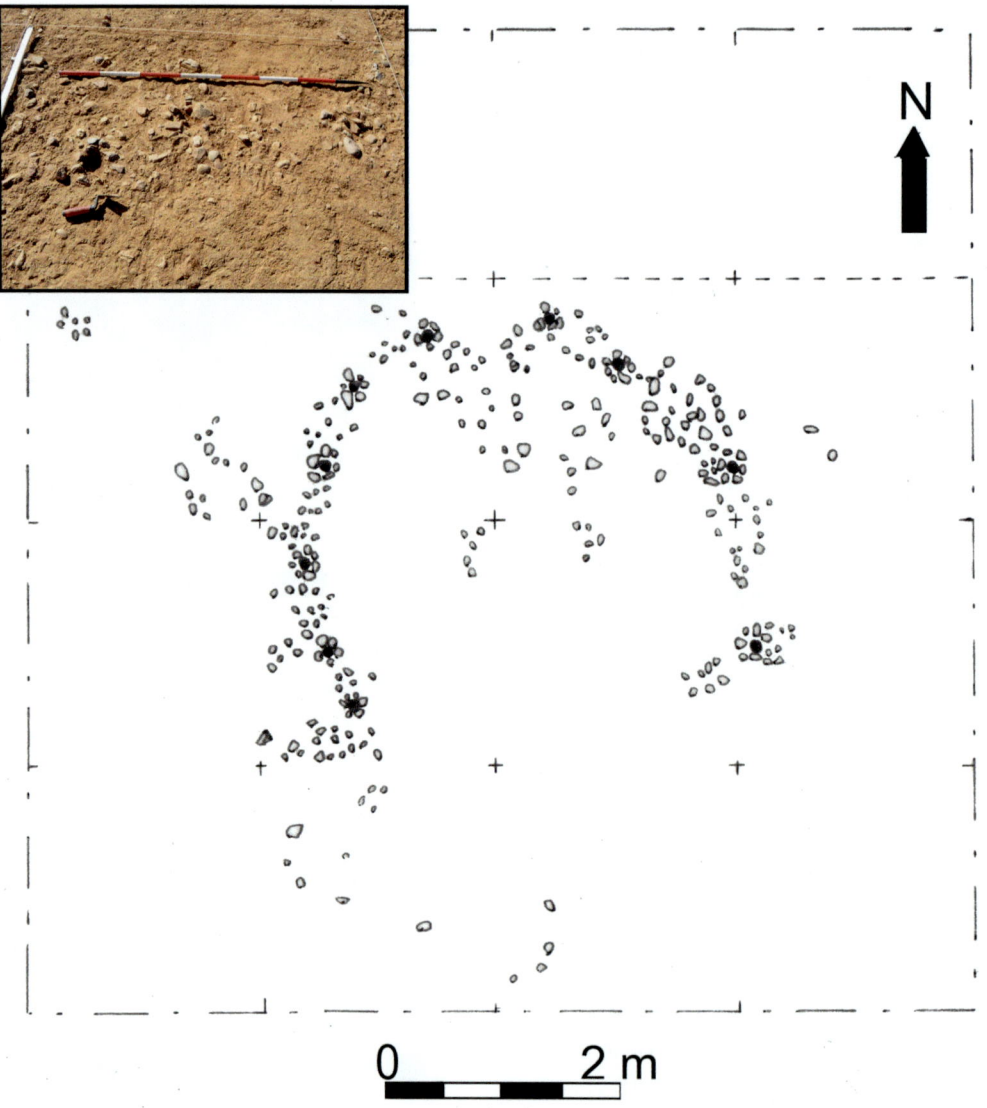

FIGURE 41: REMAINS OF A LARGE CIRCULAR HUT OR FENCE DELIMITED BY POST HOLES FROM EXCAVATION UNIT IX AT SITE UA 53.

from the earlier Gash Group sites, is only supported by the discovery of a possible wall in a test pit at site N 120 (Shiner *et al.* 1971: 396). Although, so far no structures to be ascribed to the Jebel Mokram Group were identified at Mahal Teglinos (K 1) except for some pits, the settlement there may have represented a permanent village, as suggested by the concentration of materials and by the thickness of the Jebel Mokram Group strata in the western sector of the site, whose extension is ca. 4 hectares (Fattovich 1989b: 253). There, the occurrence of a concentration of ceramic trays ca. 40cm in diameter and reminiscent of the ethnographic Ethio-Eritrean *mesob*, used in the consumption of unleavened bread, was recorded (Manzo nd.a) (Figure 42).

No tombs of this culture were identified except perhaps for some badly eroded graves later than the Gash Group occupation at Mahal Teglinos (K 1), with body with flexed legs, sometimes with the head on a stone, and grave goods consisting only of personal ornaments, some of them in *faïence*, whose superstructure was completely obliterated by erosion, except for few surviving remains of stone circles (Fattovich 1989 b: 233, 1993a: 230, 264; Fattovich, Manzo and Usai 1994: 16; Manzo nd.a) (Figure 43), and possibly for some heavily plundered tombs marked by tumuli in the northeastern sector of site UA 53 (Manzo *et al.* 2012: 9-12, 19-20).

As regards the economy of this culture, palaeobotanical collections suggest that wild millet, *Ziziphus spina-christi*, cowpea, as well as wild and domesticated sorghum were exploited (Alemseged Beldados 2015: 79-80, Table 8.2; Alemseged Beldados and Costantini 2011; Costantini *et al.* 1983: 18) (Table 1). Freshwater fish from natural pools seasonally created by rains and streams continued to be exploited, while, of course, herding continued to be crucial, as shown by remains of ovicaprines and specially of cattle (Gautier and Van Neer 2006: 229-230, Table 6) (Table 2).

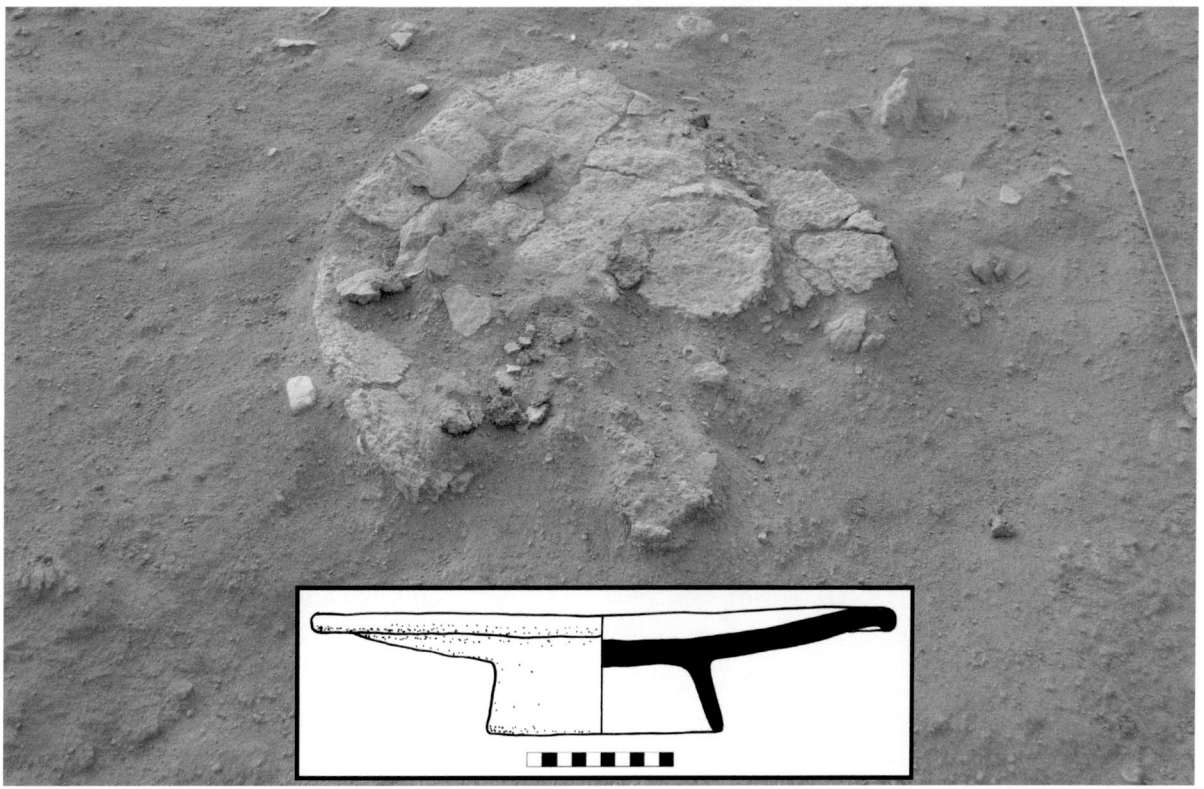

Figure 42: fragment of a large footed ceramic tray in situ in excavation unit VI at site Mahal Teglinos (K 1) and its reconstruction (scale in the image showing the reconstruction in cm).

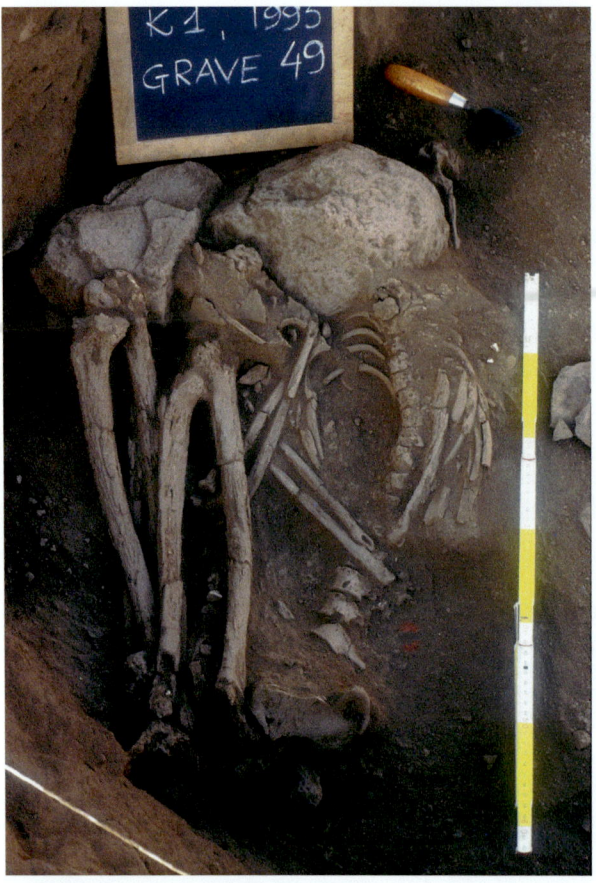

FIGURE 43: TOMB CONTAINING A BODY WITH FLEXED LEGS AND THE HEAD ON A STONE LIKELY TO DATE TO JEBEL MOKRAM GROUP TIMES IN EXCAVATION UNIT BPLF-Z/BPQA-E AT SITE MAHAL TEGLINOS (K 1).

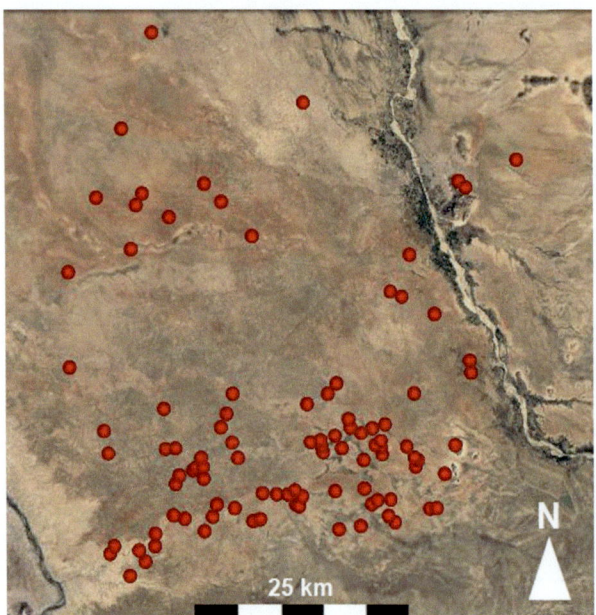

FIGURE 44: MAP SHOWING THE DISTRIBUTION OF THE JEBEL MOKRAM GROUP SITES BETWEEN THE ATBARA AND THE GASH RIVERS (PLOTTED ON GOOGLE EARTH SATELLITE IMAGE).

In terms of the settlement pattern, the smaller sites of this phase were scattered in the steppe between the Gash and the Atbara rivers, mainly close to the streams crossing the Shurab el-Gash area, while the largest ones are located closer to the Gash (Fattovich 1989a: 495, 1990a: 19-20, 1991a: 108-109; Manzo *et al.* 2012: 45; Marks and Fattovich 1989: 456; Marks and Sadr 1988: 79-80; Sadr 1988: 392, 395, 1991: 47) (Figure 44), with only a single site, N 100, recorded on the western bank of the Atbara (Shiner *et al.* 1971: 411). Also in this case like for the Gash Group the structured and articulated -although less than in the previous phase- settlement pattern was regarded as evidence of a certain degree of social hierarchy (Sadr 1991: 67-68 see also Fattovich, Sadr and Vitagliano 1988-1989: 344). A Jebel Mokram Group site, SEG 9, possibly going back to the latest phases of this culture, may have had a specialized function as more than 100 hearths were recorded on its surface (Fattovich 1990a: 21; Fattovich, Sadr and Vitagliano 1988-1989: 344). In general, it should be stressed that the larger sites of the Jebel Mokram Group were usually located alongside khors crossing the steppe and that the increasing dispersion of the sites in the steppe may suggest for this phase a bigger economic emphasis on the pastoral component (Marks and Sadr 1988: 80-81; Sadr 1991: 53, 61-63). This view is also supported by the archaeozoological evidence, showing that a constant trend to the increase of the frequency of cattle bones among the livestock already started in Gash Group times continued in Jebel Mokram Group too (Table 4). Also the remains of possible corrals perhaps used for keeping cattle and recorded on some of the smaller Jebel Mokram Group sites may indirectly confirm the relevance of livestock breeding in this culture (Sadr 1990: 73-74, Fig. 8).

3.3 Between Kush and Egypt

As previously stressed, several elements point to the presence of links between the Gash Group culture of Eastern Sudan and the Kerma ancien and Kerma moyen assemblages in Upper Nubia, but also with the C-Group of Lower Nubia, Pan-Grave as well as with Egypt (see above 3.1 *The Gash Group*).

As far as the Nubian and Nubian-like sherds are concerned, in general, the exotic sherds found in Gash Group assemblages can be ascribed to bowls, cups, and, more rarely, small bottles or flasks. Of course these typological differences in the Nubian materials found in Eastern Sudan may point to different kinds of relationships and may have different meanings. The dark gray polished bottles, a well-known type of Kerma moyen and Kerma classique vessels, found in Gash Group settlement assemblages may have been imported as containers for liquid materials (Manzo 2012: 79). Given their dimensions and the restricted necked shape, they may have contained prized liquids, possibly oils/perfumes. On the contrary the cups and bowls were most likely used in food preparation and consumption, and they were collected both in settlement and funerary contexts of the Gash Group (Manzo 2012: 79, see also Manzo 1997: 81). It is very likely that most of these cups and bowls of Nubian type were locally produced and this may point to relations not involving the circulation of vessels, but the adoption of styles and possibly the exchange of potters, i.e. the exchange of women, if we admit that also in ancient Sudan like in several traditional contexts in Africa ceramic production was a female task (Gosselain 1998: 103; MacEachern 1998: 123), a situation similar to the one proposed for explaining the diffusion of ceramic styles also in other phases of the Sudanese history (Manzo 2012: 79, see also Manzo 1997: 81). Nevertheless, the fact that sometimes a direct imitation by local potters of imported tableware brought to Eastern Sudan from Nubia could take place remains also possible in light of the above described double tomb with skeletons with legs in contracted position and associated with a Kerma ancien I/C-Group Ib vessel dating to the last centuries of the 3rd millennium BC (see above 3.1 *The Gash Group*). Actually, the distinctiveness of this tomb from the local ones strongly suggests that it should be ascribed to an individual from Upper Nubia for some reason buried in Eastern Sudan. Nevertheless, also the adoption by local people of Eastern Sudan of an articulated set of Kerma funerary traits such as the position of the body, the multiple burial -however also recorded in some Gash Group tombs (see above 3.1 *The Gash Group*)- and the typology of the associated vessel cannot be certainly ruled out, as may have happened in the case of the red ochre, a well-known feature of the Kerma graves in the Fourth Cataract area also characterizing some of the earliest Gash Group graves in the eastern cemetery (see above 3.1 *The Gash Group*).

Whatever the explanation for the occurrence of these Upper Nubian cultural elements in the region is, the interaction may have taken place in the framework of the seasonal movements involving the groups settled on the southern fringes of the Kerma area, a possibility also supported by the specific links remarked between the materials of Kerma type from Eastern Sudan and the ones of the Kerma sites in the Fourth Cataract area, i.e. the so-called Old Kush variant of the Kerma culture (see above 3.1 *The Gash Group* and also Manzo 2012: 77-78; Manzo 2014a: 1150-1151). Interestingly, it was suggested that the Kerma groups of the region of the Fourth Cataract may have adopted an apparently more and more generalized pastoral and perhaps mobile style of life at the very end of the 3rd-beginning of the 2nd millennium BC (Paner 2014: 62). On the other hand, as previously stressed, the occurrence of the closed vessels of Kerma type, although rare, may suggest that in that framework of contacts also the exchange of commodities took place between Eastern Sudan and Upper Nubia, also considering the fact that those vessels can be regarded as quite unusual in the Fourth Cataract area, while they occur at Kerma proper. The adoption of similar administrative devices such as the mushroom shaped seals both in Gash Group assemblages of Eastern Sudan and Kerma ancien and Kerma moyen assemblages of Kerma may confirm that contacts with the capital of Kush itself may have taken place too. Moreover, this last specific element may point out that those contacts may have been related to the exchange of commodities and their management.

It should be remarked that the Gash Group elements in Upper Nubian Kerma assemblages are curiously rare, and anyway limited to fragments of bowls and cups, as in the case of a bowl with a rim band consisting of a double row of finger impressions from a Fourth Cataract Kerma moyen -or Old Kush II- cemetery (see above 3.1 *The Gash Group*). Such items, like in the case of the fragments of Gash Group bowls and cups found in the Sudanese Eastern Desert, may have arrived like some Kerma bowls and cups in Eastern Sudan through the seasonal or occasional movements of people, or may have been locally made in Upper Nubia, perhaps again due to the exchange of women. Even if in both cases in the same framework also commodities from Eastern Sudan may have reached Upper Nubia, it should be remarked that the evidence of traded goods from Eastern Sudan in Upper Nubia is completely absent. Nevertheless, this evidence may have disappeared from the archaeological record because Eastern Sudan may have exported mainly un-potted, raw perishable materials and commodities, such as ebony, aromatic resins, ivory, live animals and animal skins, as well as easily reusable materials such as gold (see above 1.4 *The resources*).

Interestingly, the relations centered on Upper Nubia and involving not only the Gash Group of Eastern Sudan but also the contemporary cultures of Wadi Howar (Jesse *et al.* 2004: 158) and of the Eastern Desert (Manzo 2012: 81) emerging from the archaeological evidence mainly dating to the late 3rd-early 2nd millennium BC, represents the complementary African side of a wide network extending to the north up to the Mediterranean whose existence is suggested both by finds in the Kerma cemeteries in the Fourth Cataract area (Paner 2014: 67), and by finds from the cemetery of the capital of Kush itself (Bonnet 1997: 107). This network centered on Kerma may have certainly resulted from habits such as seasonal movements of pastoral groups, imaginable mainly towards the regions east, west and south of Upper Nubia, as well as from economic links connected to the exchange of commodities. Nevertheless the network may also have forged alliances and relations of solidarity between groups based in Upper Nubia and the groups of the regions west, east and south of it. Of course, when the elites of these groups were involved, these relations also had a political connotation and may have created a broad network of alliances centered on the most powerful and central element of the network itself, whose wideness and complexity was perhaps going to be expressed by the Kerma classique monumental structures of typically African outline excavated in the last years at Dukki Gel (Bonnet 2013: 816-817). For the earlier phases, textual documents such as the stele of general Mentuhotep from Buhen, dating to year 18 in the reign of Senwsert I (c. 1956-1911 BC, according to Shaw ed. 2000: 483) and listing several southern countries, possible members of an alliance headed by Kush (Obsomer 2007: 60-63), may already depict the early stages of such a kind of process.

On the other hand, in Gash Group times Eastern Sudan seems to have established close ties also with Egypt, as suggested by the recent discovery of ceramic materials imported from First Intermediate Period and Middle Kingdom Egypt in Gash Group assemblages (see above 3.1 *The Gash Group*). Remarkably, the identification of Eastern Sudan with Punt or a part of it was suggested, not only on the basis of its location in or near the areas of occurrence of several raw materials imported to Egypt from that region (see above 1.4 *The resources*), but also because already in the first years of the archaeological investigations of the site of Mahal Teglinos (K 1) some Egyptian sherds were collected there while, few years ago, Gash Group pottery was discovered at Mersa/Wadi Gawasis, in the Middle Kingdom harbor to the land of Punt (see above 3.1 *The Gash Group*; see also Fattovich 1991d, 1996). Moreover, for the first time, the recent discovery of Egyptian materials not only at Mahal Teglinos (K 1), but also in a further site of the region such as JAG 1 allows us to put the otherwise exceptional collections of Egyptian pottery from Mahal Teglinos (K 1) in a broader regional context.

As far as Mahal Teglinos (K 1) is concerned, in particular, a concentration of Egyptian sherds was discovered in the last years in its central sector, made of a specific typology of Marl A3 jars dating to the First Intermediate Period-early Middle Kingdom, contrasting with the rarity of this type at Kerma, moreover in association with a Nile B1 fabric dish, in turn a type completely lacking at Kerma (see above 3.1 *The Gash Group* and Manzo nd.b). These differences in the assemblages of Egyptian imports in Eastern Sudan and Upper Nubia may suggest that they resulted from different networks of circulation and that Egyptian materials could arrive in Eastern Sudan not only via the Nile valley, as it could be easily imagined, but also via the Eastern Desert and the Red Sea coast, i.e. regions that may have been touched by the Egyptian maritime expeditions organized since the Old Kingdom to reach the land of Punt through the Red Sea (see e.g. Espinel 2011: 126-131, 188-189). In particular, the occurrence at Mahal Teglinos (K 1) of Red Sea shells widely used in the production of personal ornaments as well as of some sherds imported from southern Arabia (see above 3.1 *The Gash Group*) strongly suggests that in Gash Group times Eastern Sudan had relations with the Red Sea coast, perhaps again thanks to the seasonal movements of livestock breeders towards the coast, similar to those still characterizing the region today (Fattovich 2006-2007: 89). The possibility that Eastern Sudan was in contact with the Red Sea coast may somehow be supported by the discovery of monoliths not far from Aqiq, typologically evocative of the ones discovered at Mahal Teglinos (K 1) (Fattovich 2006-2007: 92), but unfortunately so far they were not systematically investigated.

As regards the relationships with Upper Nubia and with Egypt, the exceptional role the site of Mahal Teglinos (K 1) may have played in those dynamics emerges not only from the concentration of imports and exotic materials characterizing the site, which may indeed result from randomness of sampling and from the intensive investigations conducted there, but mainly from the dimensions of the site itself, and even from the occurrence of several contemporary cemeteries there, also characterized by the coexistence of different funerary customs (see above 3.1 *The Gash Group*). This, together with the ceremonial food preparation and consumption area, where the Egyptian imports seem to be concentrated, may support the hypothesis that the site may have represented a crucial place for the establishment of relationships between different local groups, whose presence is perhaps demonstrated by the variety of the funerary customs recorded in the cemeteries (see above 3.1 *The Gash Group*), and where perhaps interactions with foreigners took place too. This hypothesis may also be supported by the apparently isolated position of the site in the settlement pattern of the Gash Group (see above 3.1 *The Gash Group*) and by the occurrence of specific monuments such as the funerary stelae, so far not recorded in the other known Gash Group sites between the Gash and the Atbara rivers and in the Gash delta.

3.4 In the *aktionsradius* of the Pan-Grave

As it was previously remarked, many parallelisms with the Pan-Grave culture of Lower Nubia and Upper Egypt characterize the ceramic corpus of the Jebel Mokram Group of Eastern Sudan (see above 3.2 *The Jebel Mokram Group* and Sadr 1987: 270-279). It should be stressed that the occurrence of these Pan-Grave elements in Eastern Sudan is also crucial for our general understanding of the Pan-Grave culture, traditionally related to the peoples of the Eastern Desert (see e.g. Bietak 1966: 70-71, 76), but whose relation with the Eastern Desert and its inhabitants was later on put into doubt because no Pan-Grave sites were apparently recorded in some specific sectors of the Eastern Desert such as the Wadi Gabgaba and Wadi Allaqi where -unsystematic- surveys were conducted (Sadr, Castiglioni and Castiglioni 1995: 226; see also Näsr 2012: 81). Nevertheless, the admittedly patchy evidence represented by more recent identification of sites with Pan-Grave materials in the Eastern Desert itself, as well as by the occurrence of Pan-Grave elements in the Kerma cemeteries of the Fourth Cataract area seems to support the traditional view and at least partially fills the gap between the Lower Nubian and Egyptian sites with Pan-Grave elements and the ones in the Jebel Mokram Group pottery of Eastern Sudan (Manzo 2012: 80-81).

The recent investigations on the Jebel Mokram Group in Eastern Sudan and in particular the re-assessment of its chronology, with a beginning not around 1500 BC, as previously thought, but around 1800 BC (see above 3.2 *The Jebel Mokram Group*) also adds new elements to the reconstruction of more general dynamics leading to the appearance of Pan-Grave elements, in light of what has been said, admittedly originating somewhere in the Eastern Desert, also in Upper Egypt, Lower Nubia and in the Fourth Cataract region, defining a sphere of action that M. Bietak termed *aktionsradius* (Bietak 1966:

70). It should be stressed that the new absolute chronology, not only makes the earliest phase of the Jebel Mokram Group roughly contemporary with the Pan-Grave sites in Upper Egypt and Lower Nubia (see Bietak 1968: 150-157), but also with some Pan-Grave occurrences in the Kerma classique -Old Kush III- assemblages in the Fourth Cataract area in association with typical materials of that region (Emberling *et al.* 2014: 332-334, Pl. 11; Emberling and Williams 2010: 33–35, Fig. 31-32; Paner 2014: 74, Pl. 32). Actually, if, according the old chronology, the appearance in Eastern Sudan of the Jebel Mokram Group 300 years later than the Pan-Grave elements in the Nile valley could be explained by a more accurate Egyptian control of the access to the valley of groups from the Eastern Desert established in New Kingdom times, that may have led to the adoption of different patterns of seasonal movements by the inhabitants of the Eastern Desert from a certain point onwards, now the fact that the contemporary appearance of Pan-Grave elements in Upper Egypt, Lower Nubia, the Fourth Cataract region and Eastern Sudan seems proven completely changes our perspective. Moreover, it should also be emphasized that while in Upper Egypt and in Lower Nubia the Pan-Grave presence is represented by well delimited concentrations of typical tombs characterized by the distinctive material culture and funerary ritual, suggesting the presence of groups from the Eastern Desert, and some elements may suggest a somehow similar situation in Eastern Sudan at least in Jebel Mokram Group times (see below), in the Fourth Cataract region we are dealing with single Pan-Grave elements in otherwise typical Kerma assemblages, suggesting only contacts with the Eastern Desert and its inhabitants.

Apparently, all this may suggest that something happened around 1800 BC favoring the presence of and the contacts with groups from the Eastern Desert in the regions around it. This may have been related to a change in the pattern of seasonal movements of the inhabitants of the Eastern Desert that were now interacting more regularly with some sectors of the Nile valley, and to the south, with Eastern Sudan. Actually, the environmental deterioration, suggested by some passages of the Semna dispatches mentioning drought and famines in the Eastern Desert (Smither 1945: 9, dispatch 5), precisely dating to the reign of Amenemhat III (c. 1831-1786 BC according to Shaw ed. 2000: 483; see also Obsomer 2007: 72 and note 118), and almost in the same phases perhaps also evident in Eastern Sudan (see above 1.3 *The present and past environment*), may explain this change that may have led to a more active involvement of the inhabitants of the Eastern Desert in symbiotic economic relationships with the surrounding regions. Moreover, from the late 12th-early 13th Dynasty onwards (see Bietak 1968: 117), this process, although possibly originating from environmental problems, may have also been related to specific situations in the Nile valley, like for example the increasing use of groups from the Eastern Desert as labor force in Egypt, where they were perhaps also involved in the management of trade and the exploitation mines in the Eastern Desert (Espinel 2011: 233-234; Näsr 2012: 85; Weschenfelder 2014: 360, 362-363). Finally, from a certain point onwards, after the 12th Dynasty, the possible weakening of the Egyptian monitoring system against the infiltration of groups from the desert in the region of the Egyptian border in Nubia and the increased autonomy of Lower Nubia itself may have favored the presence of groups from the Eastern Desert in the Nile valley (Török 2009: 96-100; Tyson Smith 2003: 76; see also Espinel 2011: 231-232). More to the south, the increasing extension of the economic and political sphere of influence of the kingdom of Kush at the passage between Kerma moyen and Kerma classique (Bonnet 2014: 81-83; Valbelle 2014: 107) was perhaps a favorable framework to the establishment of mutual ties with the inhabitants of the Eastern Desert. Archaeologically these links are made evident not only by the previously mentioned occurrence of Pan-Grave remains in the Kerma classique cemeteries in the Fourth Cataract region, i.e. the strategic part of Upper Nubia closer to the sea and from where crucial tracks penetrating the Eastern Desert such as the Korosko road start, but also by the availability to the Kerma people of gold, gemstones and Red Sea shells, which were obtained in and via the Eastern Desert (Manzo 2012: 76, 82). The kingdom of Kush may have established an indirect control on some parts of the Eastern Desert based on a network of alliances rather than a more rigid administrative and even military control, like was perhaps also the Egyptian strategy according to the Semna dispatches. Nevertheless, this specific point certainly needs further investigations, as some evidence of a more direct involvement of the kingdom of Kush in the Eastern Desert has started being available at least for Kerma classique times, like in the case of the Kerma fort located on the tracks leading to the gold mining regions of the Eastern Desert (Bonnet and Reinold 1993: 20) and of a hieroglyphic inscription perhaps mentioning the name of a king of Kush recorded in a site on the Korosko road (Davies 2014: 35-36). Whatever it is, the extension of the political sphere of influence of the kingdom of Kush to the Eastern Desert and its inhabitants during the Second Intermediate Period is also supported by the well-known painted inscription from the tomb of Sebeknakht at El-Kab, where a Kushite raid in Upper Egypt with the support of Wawat, Khenthennefer, Punt and, precisely, the Medjaw is described (Davies 2003: 52).

Returning to Eastern Sudan, as far as the relations between Pan-Grave and Jebel Mokram Group are concerned, it is true that Pan-Grave elements were already occurring in late Gash Group assemblages (see above 3.1 *The Gash Group* and Manzo 1997: 79-80), but the Pan-Grave elements in the Jebel Mokram Group pottery can be hardly explained only the by continuation of the interactions with the Eastern Desert already started in Gash Group times, because of the overwhelming number of Pan-Grave ceramic traits characterizing the Jebel Mokram Group pottery (Sadr 1987: 272, 280) and of the rapidity characterizing the stylistic change in the pottery at the passage between Gash Group and Jebel Mokram Group (see also Sadr 1990: 69). The type of vessels in the Jebel Mokram Group assemblages characterized by Pan-Grave traits may give some information on this process. The fact that they are mainly bowls and cups likely to have been used in the preparation and consumption of food suggests that this kind of interaction may have been related to the movement of people rather than of potted commodities -even if this cannot certainly exclude the exchange of un-potted commodities taking place in the meantime. Moreover, the sudden quantitative abundance of the Pan-Grave traits may support the hypothesis that groups of people were for some reasons moving from the Eastern Desert into Eastern Sudan.

In turn, this may be explained either by a migration around *c.* 1800 BC or by a newly established pattern of regular and repeated seasonal movements of mobile livestock herders (see also Sadr 1987: 280-282, 286-287) allowing a more intense interaction and possibly even a merging between groups from the Eastern Sudan and others from the Eastern Desert. Both the migration and the new pattern of seasonal movements may be related to the above described environmental changes affecting the Eastern Desert. Moreover, both models may also be in agreement with the increasing relevance of the cattle breeding, suggested for this phase by the archaeozoological data associated with Jebel Mokram Group assemblages, as well as with the increasing seasonal mobility of at least a part of the population of Eastern Sudan, perhaps emerging from the study of the Jebel Mokram Group settlement pattern, characterized by a large number of sites located in the pasture area to be interpreted for their small dimensions and thickness of the stratigraphic deposit as seasonal camps (see above 3.2 *The Jebel Mokram Group*). Also, the decreasing average dimensions and wall thickness of the vessels from Gash Group to Jebel Mokram Group (Sadr 1990: 70-71) may be interpreted as a feature related to an easier portability of the vessels fitting well in a context characterized by an increased mobility.

Of course, some other ceramic traits of the Jebel Mokram Group ceramic production seem related to the earlier regional tradition (see above 3.2 *The Jebel Mokram Group* and Sadr 1987: 273, 1990: 70), and this may reflect the merging of the foreign and the local ceramic traditions. Nevertheless, it is indubitable that in this new situation the dominant cultural reference was represented by the Pan-Grave tradition (see also Sadr 1990: 82), as shown by the fact that almost all the cups used presumably in food and drink consumption, activities eminently related to the manifestation of identity (see Tyson Smith 2003: 44-46), are exclusively of Pan-Grave type, while the typical rim banded cups and bowls with red slipped lip characterizing the latest phases of the Gash Group almost completely disappear. Indeed, it is really a pity that so far very few data were collected on the Jebel Mokram Group funerary traditions, a further field potentially very informative in the perspective of the study of identity (Tyson Smith 2003: 38-39). Nevertheless, also the few available data, showing the abandonment of the extended supine position and the apparently generalized adoption of the contracted one, as well as the end in the use of funerary stelae supplanted -perhaps already at the end of the Gash Group- by circles of stones possibly originally delimiting tumuli (see above 3.2 *The Jebel Mokram Group*), seem to suggest a certain degree of discontinuity from the earlier phase.

All this certainly does not mean that the local culture was completely supplanted by the new one. As far as the subsistence economy and perhaps the culinary traditions are concerned, the relevance of domesticated sorghum already evident in Gash Group times continued and most likely even increased in the Jebel Mokram Group agro-pastoral adaptive system (see above 3.2 *The Jebel Mokram Group*), perhaps also thanks to the fitness of this cereal to more arid conditions. Most likely some continuity can also be identified in the general economic role of Eastern Sudan in the macro-regional setting. Actually, while the continuity in the involvement of Eastern Sudan in long-distance networks was so far only hypothesized in the lack of any clear evidence of contacts e.g. with Egypt (Sadr 1987: 273, 1990: 80), harshly contrasting with the data available for the Gash Group, in the last years Egyptian sherds and other elements pointing to contacts with Egypt were also discovered in Jebel Mokram Group assemblages (see above 3.2 *The Jebel Mokram Group* and Manzo nd.b), and their number may likely increase with the intensification of research on this phase. For this reason, in some New Kingdom texts, the association between the Medjaw people, an ethnic label traditionally related to the Eastern Desert and the Pan-Grave culture itself (see e.g. Säve-Söderbergh 1941: 139; see also Giuliani 2004: 286, but see Bietak 1966: 68), and the land of Punt (Bietak 1966: 78; Giuliani 2004: 286; Sadr 1987: 287) may be considered very intriguing, as was previously suggested on the basis of the evidence dating to Gash Group times that Eastern Sudan may have been part of this very important trade partner of Pharaonic Egypt (see above 3.3 *Between Kush and Egypt*). As far as the relations with Upper Nubia are concerned, they may have continued also at the beginning of this phase, before the establishment of the Egyptian control on the Nile valley up to the Fourth Cataract region, thanks to the possible increased interaction between the Eastern Desert and its inhabitants and the kingdom of Kush in Kerma classique times (see above).

Therefore, to sum up, the occurrence of Pan-Grave elements in the Jebel Mokram Group assemblages of Eastern Sudan can be considered as related to more intense interactions with the Eastern Desert and to a more active involvement of the inhabitants of the Eastern Desert in the relations with the surrounding regions also evident at a more general level in Egypt and Nubia. All this may be in turn originated by specific environmental factors, and also related to the still little understood process of increment of the political sphere of action of the kingdom of Kush to the east and to the southeast of Upper Nubia. Both of these factors may have affected not only the Eastern Desert, but also Eastern Sudan itself. Interestingly, while in Upper Egypt, Lower Nubia and in the Fourth Cataract area all this may have ended c. 1500 BC, as shown by the disappearance of the Pan-Grave elements in the archaeological record, perhaps as a consequence of the acculturation of the groups from the Eastern Desert settled in the Nile valley (but see De Souza 2013, p. 117), but also of a changed political and administrative situation emerging at the beginning of the New Kingdom, possibly preventing further infiltrations and arrivals in the Nile valley, apparently Pan-Grave traits lasted longer in Eastern Sudan, which remained unaffected by the direct Egyptian expansion and its effects.

Chapter 4
The transition to nomadism (c. 1000 BC-AD 1500)

4.1 The Hagiz Group

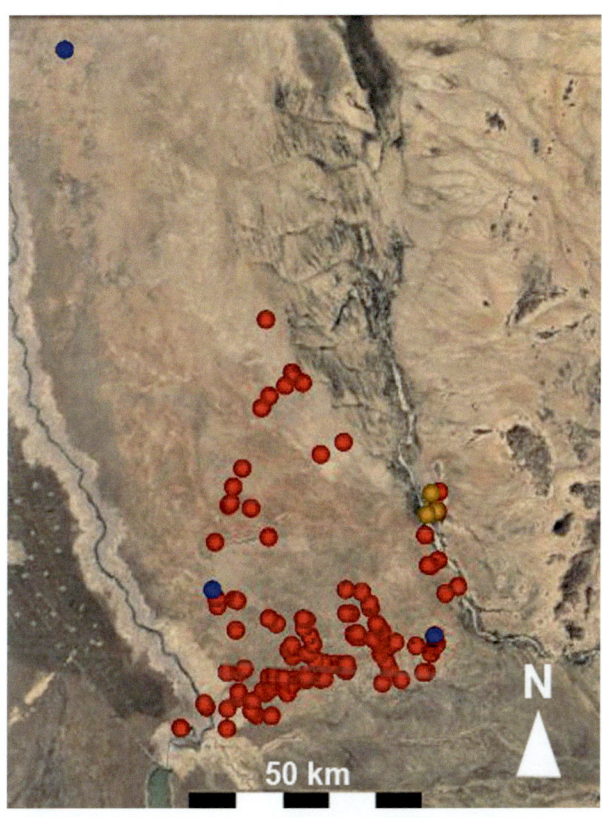

FIGURE 45: MAP SHOWING THE DISTRIBUTION OF THE HAGIZ GROUP SITES MARKED BY RED DOTS, OF THE POST-MEROITIC SITES MARKED BY BLUE DOTS, AND OF THE KHATMIYA GROUP SITES MARKED BY YELLOW DOTS (PLOTTED ON GOOGLE EARTH SATELLITE IMAGE).

The Hagiz Group sites, often apparently deliberately located on top on earlier sites, usually characterized by the limited dimensions and a very thin deposit, suggesting that they originated from small temporary camps or even single temporary compounds, are scattered between the Atbara and the Gash and can be divided into two groups, the first one in the sector of the Khor Marmadeb, the second north of the Khor Qaratit, around possible ancient and seasonally available pools originated by the rains in the plain or at the base of outcrops, while larger sites, perhaps with more consistent structures suggesting permanent and/or repeated occupations, may have been located near the Gash delta and near Jebel Abu Gamal, at site JAG 1 (Fattovich 1989a: 497, 1989d: 799, 1990a: 22, 1991a: 111; Fattovich, Sadr and Vitagliano 1988-1989: 344-346; Marks and Fattovich 1988: 81; Manzo 2016: 194-195; Manzo *et al.* 2011: 13-15, 2012: 45; Sadr 1988: 392, 395, 1991: 48-50) (Figure 45). In particular, at JAG 1 the stone foundations of possible huts have been recorded in association with materials of the Hagiz Group and also some rock shelters at the foot of the granitic hill may have been opportunistically used at that time (Manzo 2016: 194-195) (Figure 46).

The ceramic production, mainly consisting of undecorated vessels, also includes types closely related to the earlier phases of the Atbai Ceramic Tradition, such as bowls and cups with rim bands and crossing bands of oblique incised lines recalling the Gash Group and Jebel Mokram Group respectively (Figure 47 a), together with a less accurate type of scraped ware characterized by shallow incisions (Figure 47 b) and impressed and pinched rims, as well as mat impressed ware (Figure 47 c). The pink-orange fabric characterized by fiber vegetal temper is a very distinctive marker of the Hagiz Group (Sadr 1991: 48), making the vessels lighter (Figure 47 b, d). Horizontal lop handles and vertical handles (Figure 47 d-e) represent an innovation in the regional tradition, perhaps related to an increased need of portability. Modeled knobs, impressed ledges (Figure 48 a, b) and horizontal grips with incisions (Figure 48 c) are reminiscent of pre-Aksumite vessels of northern Ethiopia and Eritrea, while the bowls with grooved ledge rims are similar to Aksumite types (Figure 48 d) (Fattovich 1989a: 497, 1989d: 799, 1990a: 22, 1991a: 111-112; Fattovich, Marks and Mohammed-Ali 1984: 187; Manzo *et al.* 2012: 65-68; Sadr 1991: 48).

In the unfortunate lack of radiocarbon dates for this culture, its suggested absolute chronology ranging from the early 1st millennium BC to the mid-1st millennium AD is only based on the above mentioned

Figure 46: remains of the stone foundations of a rounded Hagiz Group hut north of excavation unit III at site JAG 1 (scale in m).

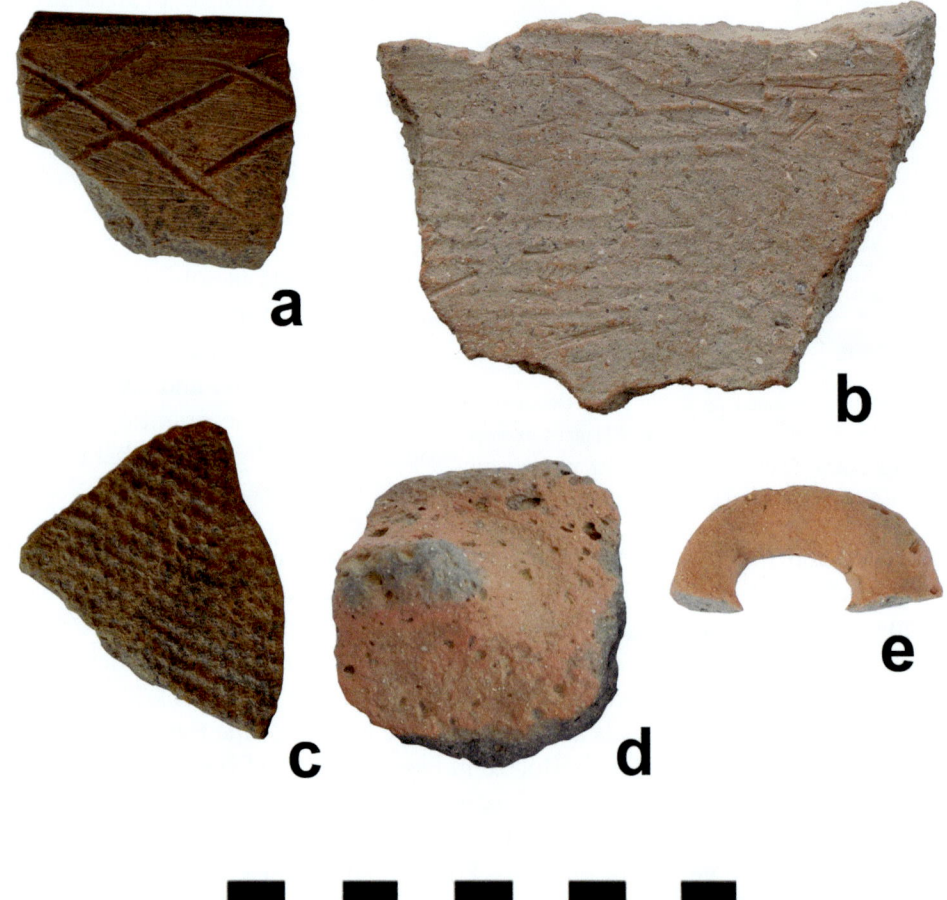

Figure 47: fragments of Hagiz Group ceramics: a) rim of a bowl with a band of oblique parallel crossing incisions from site UA 38; b) wall sherd of a vegetal tempered scraped ware vessel from site JAG 1; c) wall sherd of mat impressed ware from site UA 38; d) vegetal tempered body sherd of a vessel with vertical handle from site UA 127; e) horizontal loop handle of a vegetal tempered vessel from site UA 132 (scale in cm).

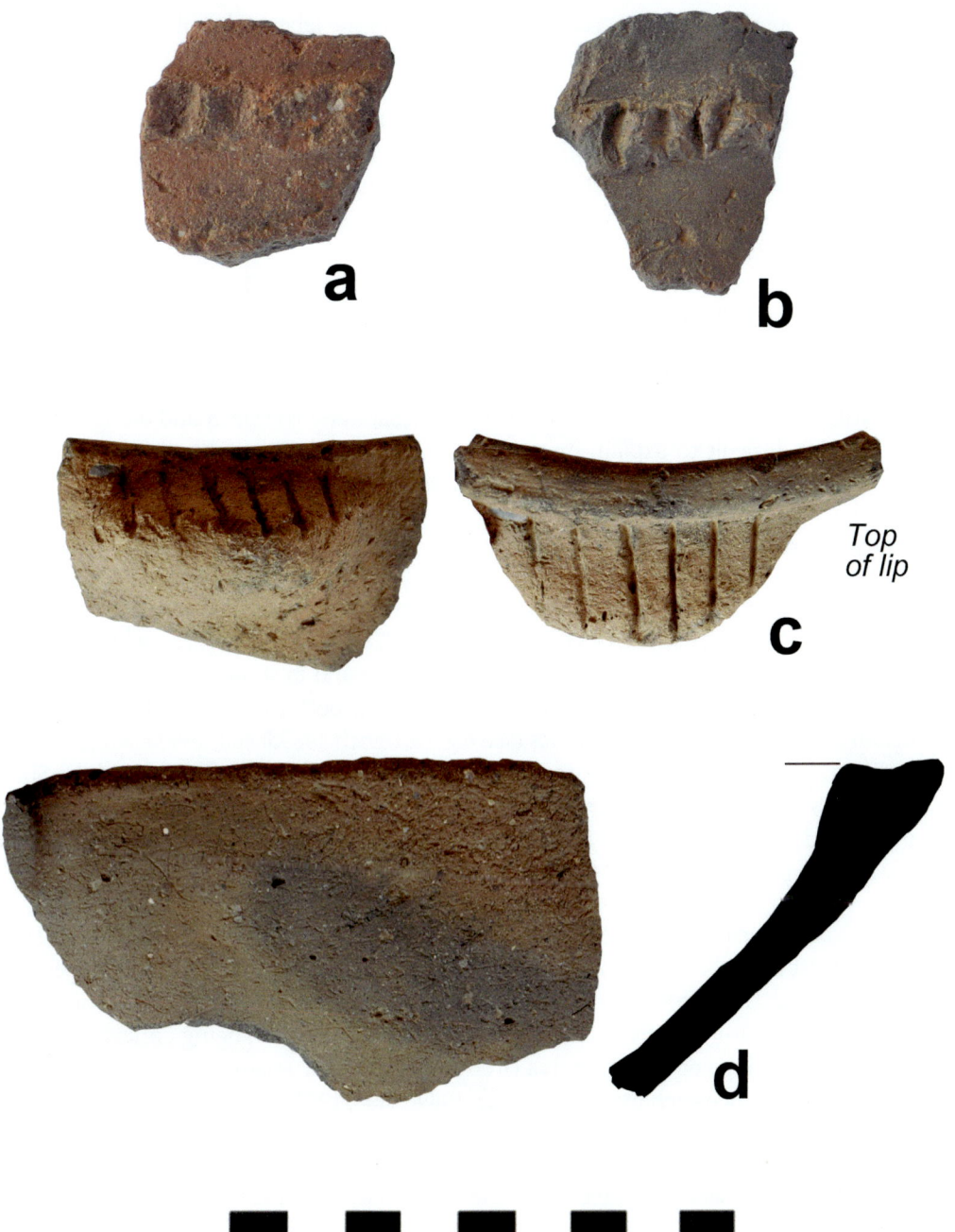

Figure 48: fragments of Hagiz Group ceramics: a-b) body sherds of vessels decorated with impressed modeled ledges from site UA 129; c) side and top view of a fragment of rim of a vegetal tempered bowl with grip with incisions on it from site UA 16; d) fragment of a flaring rim cup with a groove on the lip from site UA 21 (scale in cm).

comparisons with the ceramics of the pre-Aksumite and Aksumite cultures of the Ethiopian and Eritrean highlands, and on the occurrence in some Hagiz Group sites of Late Antique Mediterranean ribbed amphorae (Fattovich 1989a: 497, 1991a: 112; Fattovich, Marks and Mohammed-Ali 1984: 187; Manzo *et al.* 2012: 65-68) and of fragments of Khatmiya Group/Eastern Desert Ware pottery (see below 4.2 *The Khatmiya Group*). In the meantime, the above mentioned similarities in the pottery of the Hagiz Group as well as the imported materials may also point out to relationships with neighboring regions.

Hagiz Group lithics are not very different from the earlier ones of the Jebel Mokram Group, but, interestingly, almost completely lacking of the grinding stones (Sadr 1991: 49).

As far as the subsistence economy is concerned, although a systematic archaeozoological study of the remains from the contexts of this culture is still lacking, the bones of cattle seem to occur widely in the Hagiz Group assemblages (Sadr 1991: 56), suggesting the crucial role of cattle breeding, also compatible with the above mentioned characteristics of the settlement pattern of this culture (Table 2). Nevertheless, the few palaeobotanical data collected at site UA 129 may suggest that also in Hagiz Group times the exploitation of wild and domesticated sorghum and of millets continued (Alemseged Beldados 2015: 79-80, Table 8.2) (Table 1). The evidence of cultivation of domesticated crops such as the sorghum as well as of sites with more consistent structures partially modifies the view that the Hagiz Group was an eminently pastoral and nomadic culture (Sadr 1991: 56, 59), showing that an articulated agro-pastoral model may have survived at least in the Gash delta, if not in the area between the Atbara and the Gash and along the Gash. In this framework, it remains difficult to explain on purely environmental and economic grounds the fact that fertile lands along the Gash river were apparently overlooked in this phase.

4.2 The Khatmiya Group

In the absence of radiocarbon dates, the suggested absolute chronology of this culture to the 3rd-6th centuries AD is suggested by the clear link between its ceramics and the Eastern Desert Ware, a class of pottery widely occurring in the sites of the Eastern Desert of Egypt and Sudan and in some sites of Lower Nubia (Manzo 2004: 79, 2014d: 237-238, Fig. 15). Actually, the Khatmiya Group pottery -previously compared with pre-Aksumite, Aksumite and even Meroitic ceramics (see e.g. Fattovich 1989d: 800, 1990a: 23)- can now be quite safely regarded as related to the Eastern Desert Ware of the Eastern Desert of Egypt and the Sudan, and is characterized by mineral tempered cylindrical beakers and globular bowls with accurate surface treatment, impressed and incised decorations forming wavy patterns, panels alternated with undecorated zones, often highlighted by colored pastes (Manzo 2004: 77-79, Fig. 3, Pls. 4-5) (Figure 49).

Some Khatmiya Group sherds were collected on sites of the Hagiz Group (see above 4.1 *The Hagiz Group*), confirming the at least partial contemporaneity of the two cultures. Like in the assemblages of the Hagiz Group, sherds of ribbed Late Antique Mediterranean amphorae were also collected on the Khatmiya Group sites: they are relevant both from the chronological point of view, being coherent with the above proposed absolute chronology of the Khatmiya Group, and for their meaning, showing the involvement of this culture in long-distance exchanges (Fattovich 1989d: 800, 1991a: 112, 1990a: 24; Manzo 2004: 79, Pl. 6, 1-2) (Figure 50).

Unfortunately, so far no data were collected about the subsistence system of this culture.

As far as the settlement pattern is concerned, the sites of this culture are absent in the area between the Gash and the Atbara rivers, while the only five Khatmiya Group sites, apparently associated with small stone tumuli with diameter ranging from 3 to 10m and some red brick structures, seem to cluster near the Jebel Taka, as it was previously remarked (Fattovich 1989d: 799, 1990a: 23-24, 1991a: 112; Manzo 2004: 75, 2014d: 246) (Figure 45).

4.3 The-Post Meroitic sites

Although very rare, few sites with typical Post-Meroitic materials occur in Eastern Sudan. A site characterized by Post-Meroitic materials most likely associated with a cemetery with tumuli was identified in the northern part of the region, ca. 20km South of Jebel Ofreik and 20km east of the ford of Goz Regeb (Figure 51), a traditional gateway between Eastern Sudan and the Butana (Manzo 2004: 75-77), while further sites with typical Post-Meroitic materials were recently recorded north of the Khor Umm Sitebah (Manzo *et*

The transition to nomadism (c. 1000 BC–AD 1500)

Figure 49: fragments of Khatmiya Group ceramics from site K 4 (scale in cm).

Figure 50: fragments of ribbed Late Antique Mediterranean amphorae from Khatmiya Group assemblages at site K 24 B (scale in cm).

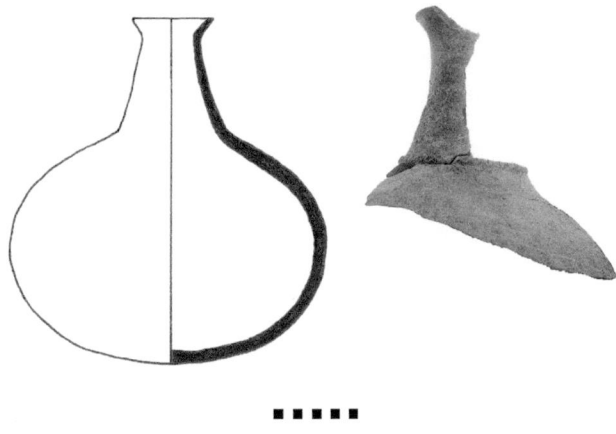

Figure 51: Post-Meroitic beer-jar vessels from a site in the area of Jebel Ofreik (scale in cm).

FIGURE 52: POST MEROITIC EVIDENCE AT SITE JAG 1: A) THE TUMULUS IN EXCAVATION UNITS I AND II DELIMITED BY A RING OF GRANITE STONES AND TOPPED BY QUARTZ PEBBLES; B) THE FUNERARY PIT WITH A BADLY DAMAGED SKELETON AT THE BASE; C) IRON ARROWHEADS FOUND AT THE BASE OF THE PIT AND IN THE NICHE; D) GLASS AND STONE BEADS FOUND AT THE BASE OF THE PIT AND IN THE NICHE (SCALE IN CM IN IMAGES C AND D).

al. 2012: 45, 68, Fig. 99) and at the foot of the Jebel Abu Gamal (Figure 45). In particular, this last site was characterized by the occurrence of large soil tumulus exceeding 10m in diameter (Fattovich 1991a: 115; Manzo 2016: 194) delimited by a ring of granite rocks and originally topped with white quartz pebbles covering funerary pits filled with stones and with a lateral niche containing skeletons in contracted position (Figure 52, a-b). There, typical iron barbed arrowheads as well as glass and stone beads were collected (Figure 52 c-d). Nevertheless, the isolation of these sites may somehow confirm that they are intrusive and may represent an occasional presence in the region of groups moving from the Butana (see Manzo 2004: 77).

Unfortunately, no data are available on the subsistence strategy of the people frequenting the Post-Meroitic sites.

4.4 Scatters of tumuli

Tumuli and stone cairns presumably dating to the 1st millennium AD, but lacking the typical Post-Meroitic or Khatmiya Group pottery to which tumuli were sometimes associated (see above 4.1 *The Hagiz Group* and 4.2 *The Khatmiya Group*) are widely scattered in the Gash delta and near Kassala, sometimes along the rocky outcrops (Fattovich 1989d: 800-802, 1991a: 114, 1993a: 227). They usually form clusters of tumuli of stones up to 20-30m in diameter (Fattovich 1989d: 800, 1990a: 24). Their chronology was suggested by a single radiocarbon date.[8]

---

[8] Fattovich 1993a: 236, Gif-6558: 1180±80 BP.

One of those tumuli, 4m in diameter, at the entrance of Mahal Teglinos (K 1) when excavated resulted to contain three superimposed successive burials, plus a more superficial intrusive one, with bodies in semi-contracted position and associated to personal ornaments such as ear rings, bone, cornelian and glass beads (Fattovich 1989b: 235, 1989d: 801, 1991a: 115, 1993a: 235). Of a second tumulus in the central sector of the site at Mahal Teglinos (K 1) only a stone cairn ca. 2m in diameter survived and marked a funerary pit containing a skeleton with contracted legs (Fattovich 1989d: 800-801, 1991a: 115) (Figure 53). At the same site, a third burial whose tumulus was completely eroded contained the contracted skeletons of an adult and a child with a bracelet (Fattovich 1989d: 801).

4.5 The Christian sites

M 6, a site characterized by black slipped ware, red polished ware, red ware with impressed ledges and incised decorative patterns among which the occurrence of crosses should be remarked, is located west of the Gash delta (Fattovich 1989d: 803, 1990a: 25, 1991a: 113, 1993a: 227). Also some red bricks characterized by engraved fishes, crosses and Greek letters were found there (Fattovich 1989d: 803, 1990a: 25). A further unpublished site with pottery

FIGURE 53: CONTRACTED SKELETON IN A TUMULUS IN THE CENTRAL SECTOR OF THE SITE AT MAHAL TEGLINOS (K 1).

characterized by incised crosses was discovered in the area of Jebel Ofreik (Figure 54). The pottery from these sites was considered as related to some productions from Soba (Fattovich 1989d: 803, 1990a: 25).

North of Kassala, not far from the paved road to Port Sudan, a cemetery was recently discovered in a sector of site UA 126 (Manzo 2013: 256). Although the attitude of the bodies, in extended position on the right flank, with the right arm along the body and the left one flexed, recalls that of Muslim graves, their orientation varies from east-west to north-south, with the head to the south or to the east. No grave goods were discovered in association with the graves, and even on the surface, only bones from eroded graves and fragments of red bricks were collected. In particular, the use of red bricks in the superstructure of some of the graves to form a kind of bench (Figure 55) is not related to Muslim habits, and may be compared to the structures characterizing some Christian cemeteries in Upper Nubia (Welsby 2002: 58-59). Interestingly, also the orientation of the body with the head to the east should not be regarded as an exclusive Muslim habit, as it is not unknown in the southern regions of Christian Nubia (Welsby 2002: 48-49), therefore an attribution to a Christian community can be proposed for this cemetery.

4.6 The Gergaf Group

This culture represents the last phase recorded in the cultural sequence of Eastern Sudan, although not a part of the Atbai Ceramic Tradition, as its pottery lacks the regional markers such as the scraped ware and the rim bands (see above 1.2 *The archaeological exploration of Eastern Sudan*). An absolute

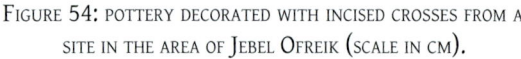

FIGURE 54: POTTERY DECORATED WITH INCISED CROSSES FROM A SITE IN THE AREA OF JEBEL OFREIK (SCALE IN CM).

FIGURE 55: BENCH MADE OF RED BRICKS MARKING A TOMB DAMAGED BY A LATER GRAVE WITH BODY IN EXTENDED POSITION VISIBLE ON THE RIGHT IN EXCAVATION UNIT II AT SITE UA 126.

chronology to the 15th-18th century AD was suggested for this culture not only on the basis of similarities between its ceramics and the ethnographic ones of the Beja inhabiting the region as well as the ones of the Funji period in the Gezira (Fattovich 1991a: 114, 127, see also Fattovich, Marks and Mohammed-Ali 1984: 187), but also of three radiocarbon dates.[9]

The Gergaf Group is characterized by heavily decorated reddish and buff bag shaped mineral and vegetal tempered vessels, with flat rims, horizontal superimposed bands of crossing oblique lines and chevrons of wavy incised lines on the upper part of the vessel, by mat impressed ware, and by lugs with an incised cross pattern (Fattovich 1991a: 114; Fattovich, Marks and Mohammed-Ali 1984: 187-188; Manzo *et al.* 2012: 69-60; Sadr 1984: 33, Fig. 1) (Figure 56, a-b).

The sites of the Gergaf Group, located in the steppes north-east of Kashm el Griba, near active streams, the Khor Marmadeb, and few kilometers north of Khor Qaratit, between the Gash and the area of Shurab el-Gash, but also in the Gash delta, are either large sites, characterized by well-delimited concentrations of material and thin stratigraphic deposit, or smaller sites always with thin stratigraphic deposit, pointing respectively to a seasonally repeated use of the spot and to a short, possibly single, occupation (Fattovich 1991a: 114; Manzo *et al.* 2012: 46; Sadr 1984: 34-35)

---

[9] See Fattovich 1991a: 114; Sadr 1984: 33, SMU 1289: 159±75 bp; Manzo *et al.* 2012: 18, Beta 311301: 280±30 bp; unpublished date Beta 428645 180±30 bp.

Figure 56: Gergaf Group ceramics: a) fragmentary decorated bag shaped mineral and vegetal tempered vessel, with flat rim and horizontal band of crossing incisions on the upper part of the vessel from site UA 35; b) fragmentary decorated bag shaped mineral and vegetal tempered vessel, with flat rim and horizontal band of crossing incisions on the upper part of the vessel from site UA 29 (scale in cm).

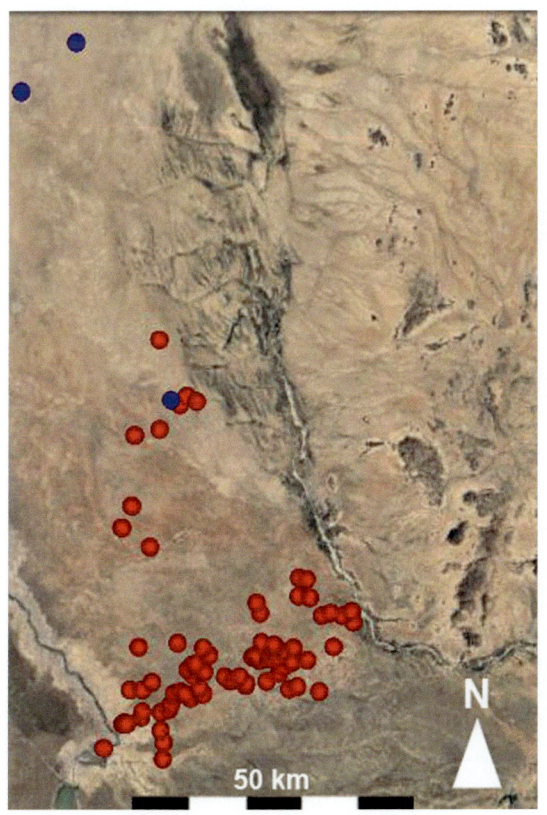

(Figure 57). The larger sites are closer to the Atbara and in the Shurab el-Gash area, the smaller ones are scattered in the plain between the rivers Gash and Atbara and this, together with the above described characteristics of the sites, suggests an agro-pastoral economy with an emphasis on the pastoral mobile component and a possible agricultural component in the more fertile areas, although unfortunately no palaeobotanical and archaeozoological data are available for this culture (Sadr 1984: 34-35).

Along the Atbara some cemeteries characterized by oblong cairns consisting of river cobbles and also by quadrangular structures were recorded (Sadr 1984: 34). A different kind of funerary structure to be ascribed to the Gergaf Group was recorded at site UA

Figure 57: map showing the distribution of the Gergaf Group sites marked by red dots, and of the sites with Christian materials marked by blue dots (plotted on Google Earth satellite image).

143, near Aroma Station, in the Gash delta: a tumulus associated to ceramic plaques bearing Arabic inscriptions with personal names, presumably that of the dead people, and to a concentration of ceramics was surrounded by graves with skeletons in semi-contracted position and with the head to the west (Manzo 2015: 234-235) (Figure 58).

As far as the type of structures recorded in the settlements is concerned, at UA 53 the postholes of an elongated hut also associated with a couple of fireplaces and somehow evocative of the ethnographic Beja tents were investigated (Manzo *et al.* 2012: 16-18) (Figure 59).

4.7 The Islamic sites

In Eastern Sudan, northeast of Kassala, along the wadi systems draining from the Red Sea hills to the Gash basin and from the Red Sea hills to the coastal plain, several sites with obviously Islamic remains also occur, although not in the region between the Gash and the Atbara. They are characterized by well-preserved funerary structures consisting of simple domed tombs and by more complex funerary structures consisting of cubic bases topped by further squared or cylindrical elements and by a dome (Paul 1952: 54-55). One of the largest sites characterized by such funerary structures is certainly Jebel Maman, where the structures cluster along the footslopes of a hill (Figure 60). Unfortunately, these sites were never properly investigated, and for this reason their chronology is unclear, although it can be reasonably fixed around the 9th-10th century for the simpler structures and in the 16th -17th century for the more elaborated ones (Fattovich 2010a: 103-104; Elsadig 2000: 38; see also Fattovich 1990a: 25).

Figure 58: Gergaf Group mound with concentration of ceramic materials possibly used for funerary offerings at site UA 143.

The transition to nomadism (c. 1000 BC-AD 1500)

Figure 59: Gergaf Group hut delimited by post holes marked by the red and white sticks in excavation unit VI of site UA 53.

Figure 60: A view of the Islamic cemetery with complex funerary structures at Jebel Maman.

Clusters of ancient cubical buildings, sometimes sustaining a further cylindrical or cubical element topped by a dome were also discovered along the footslopes of the Ethio-Eritrean highlands, east of Kassala (Fattovich 1990a: 25-26). In the same area, some sites with clusters of cubical stone buildings may also be interpreted as groups of Islamic graves, with only the lower part of the structures surviving (Fattovich 1991a: 116).

4.8 A nomadic melting pot

In light of what has been said in the previous paragraphs, from the 1st millennium BC to the mid-2nd millennium AD, Eastern Sudan seems to have been characterized by two main traits: the increasing mobility of its inhabitants, that led Sadr to consider the Hagiz Group as an archaeological expression of 'true nomads' (Sadr 1991: 59), and the coexistence, very evident mainly in the first half of the 1st millennium AD, in contiguous if not overlapping areas of contemporaneous groups characterized by different material culture and possibly style of life (Manzo 2004: 80-81). Interestingly, the adoption of a nomadic style of life was regarded alternatively as a symptom of a political and economic marginalization of the region in the macro-regional setting (Sadr 1991: 117) and as a consequence of a deeper involvement of Eastern Sudan in a systemic relationship with the neighboring regions and more specifically with the Butana and middle Nile region (Brass 2014: 266).

Actually, it should be remarked that the progressive shift to a more mobile, perhaps nomadic style of life in the 1st millennium BC is mainly evident in the Hagiz Group, a culture characterized by a strong relationship with the earlier cultural traditions of Eastern Sudan (see above 4.1 *The Hagiz Group*). As a matter of fact, from a cultural point of view, in the 1st millennium BC-first half of the 1st millennium AD, the locally rooted regional tradition continued in Eastern Sudan apparently unaffected by the flourishing of the kingdom of Kush in the Butana and in the middle Nile valley. This certainly does not mean that there were no relations between this region and the Butana, as suggested by the occurrence of some Meroitic sherds at the site of Goz Regeb,[10] just east of the Atbara, near a traditional ford. Nevertheless, nothing comparable to the sites in the Gezira suggesting more intense and prolonged interactions with the core area of the Kushite state, very evident at Sennar and Jebel Moya itself (Bradley 1992: 211-212; Brass 2016: 147-153), was so far discovered in Eastern Sudan. On the contrary, if we look at the Hagiz Group ceramic materials, beside traditional traits typical of the regional tradition, when exotic elements can be pointed out, they seem to be mainly oriented to the Ethio-Eritrean highlands (see above 4.1 *The Hagiz Group*). Moreover, it should be stressed that in the 1st millennium BC this relation between an apparently peripheral region and the pre-Aksumite core area centered in northern Ethiopia and central Eritrea was not at all passive: on the contrary it seems highly possible that Eastern Sudan contributed to the rise of the pre-Aksumite ceramic tradition, as several elements apparently related to the middle Nile valley remarked in it (see already Fattovich 1982: 78-81) may have reached the Ethio-Eritrean highlands precisely via the Atbai Ceramic Tradition (Manzo 2014b: 1154). The fact that scraped ware, a typical trait of the Atbai Ceramic Tradition, and black topped ware occur together in the same assemblages of sites on the Ethio-Eritrean highlands dating to the early 1st millennium BC, i.e. some centuries later than the pre-Aksumite pottery appeared,[11] suggests that the spread of middle Nile valley traits to northern Ethiopia and Eritrea may have taken place in the framework of increasing contacts with Eastern Sudan precisely at the beginning of the 1st millennium BC. These contacts may have been favored by the seasonal movements of the pastoral groups on the northwestern fringes of the highlands.

Interestingly, although limited in number, some objects suggesting some kind of relationship between Napatan and later on Meroitic Kush and northern Ethiopia and Eritrea, where at that time the local states of Daamat, and later on, Aksum flourished, are known (see e.g. Manzo 1998; Phillips 2014: 256-257, 259-260), while Kushite materials are completely lacking in Eastern Sudan. This fact not only suggests a scarce concern of the Kushites for Eastern Sudan, but also that the interaction related to the seasonal movements of the livestock breeders possibly explaining the similarities in the ceramic traditions of Eastern Sudan and northern Ethiopia and Eritrea was a different dynamic from the one(s) that determined the occurrence of Kushite artifacts in some pre-Aksumite and Aksumite assemblages.

The continuity in the cultural links with the Ethio-Eritrean highlands made evident by the material culture of the Hagiz Group also for the first half of the 1st millennium AD (see above 4.1 *The Hagiz*

---

[10] This emerged from a new examination of materials collected in the Eighties and kept in the university museum of the 'L'Orientale' University.
[11] This is now very evident in the ceramic sequence of Mezber, a pre-Aksumite settlement site in Eastern Tigrai investigated by a Canadian expedition of Simon Fraser University; for some preliminary remarks on this, see also Manzo 2014: 1154-1155. The publication of the ceramic sequence of Mezber will be included in the final report of the excavation, whose preparation is in progress.

Group) may be related to the continuity in a pattern of the seasonal movements by the pastoral nomadic groups inhabiting Eastern Sudan, most likely oriented north-south and not east-west. On the other hand, it should also be remarked that this pattern may somehow be precisely related to the presence of a powerful Kushite state west of the Atbara, as we cannot exclude that the east-west seasonal movements may have been prevented and somehow inhibited by such a presence. Actually, not only the rise of a powerful state in the middle Nile valley may have prevented nomadic groups based in Eastern Sudan to approach its eastern fringes, but the Kushite rulers may have perhaps exerted a kind of patronage on some nomadic groups exploiting the eastern Butana and moving up to the Atbara (Bradley 1992: 211-213). Actually, it was suggested that the patronage of the Kushite state on some groups of livestock breeders of the Butana was shown by the *hafir*-temple complexes not associated with substantial traces of settlements, and around which it was suggested that this mobile pastoral component of the Kushite state periodically grouped (Bradley 1992: 171; Hinkel 1994: 174). Unfortunately, all these aspects related to the relevance of the pastoral component in the Kushite economy remain very poorly investigated and understood. Nevertheless, as a matter of fact, such a kind of Kushite attitude towards the inhabitants of the eastern Butana may have also originated consequences in the region east of the Butana, mainly because of possible military activities in these areas already in Napatan times (see again Bradley 1992: 213) continuing up to Meroitic times, as perhaps witnessed by the well-known reliefs of Shorkaror at Jebel Qeili, and by some names of vanquished peoples listed on the eastern façade of temple M 250 at Meroe (Abdalla 1989: 383-384). These possible military campaigns may have precisely affected the patterns of mobility of the groups inhabiting Eastern Sudan and inhibited their approach to regions in the Kushite sphere of action.

Therefore, in light of what has been said, the recently proposed model of Eastern Sudan as closely linked to the Meroitic Butana and representing a kind of corridor between Meroe and the Red Sea, and through it, to the Indian Ocean, with the active involvement of its inhabitants (see Brass 2015: 266) remains for the moment unproven -as on the other hand also the suggested ties between Meroe and India recently re-proposed, and in which Eastern Sudan was again regarded to have been a crucial link on the way to the Red Sea (see Haaland 2014: 655-656 and again Brass 2015: 260-261).

Apparently, the situation in Eastern Sudan changed in the 3rd century AD, with the intensification of contacts with the peoples of the Eastern Desert, possibly represented by the Khatmiya Group sites clustering around the Jebel Taka. The limited and well-defined area of Eastern Sudan where the Khatmiya Group sites occur, may suggest that groups from the Eastern Desert penetrated this part of the region, or for some reasons settled there (Manzo 2004: 80-81; see above 4.2 *The Khatmiya Group*). Interestingly, the settlement of groups from the Eastern Desert in areas in the Aksumite sphere of influence -like perhaps Eastern Sudan was at that time- is also recorded in epigraphic sources: this was what happened to some Beja tribes after being subjugated by the Aksumite king Ezana in the mid 4th century AD (Hatke 2013: 125-127). Whatever it is, both the possibility of a forced or voluntary settlement in Eastern Sudan and that of a periodical recurrent presence in the region can be related to the well-known phase of intense activity of the groups inhabiting the Eastern Desert starting from the 3rd century AD and also affecting the Nile valley and the Red Sea coast. This increased activism of the inhabitants of the Eastern Desert may have been favored by the diffusion of the camel as livestock in that region, allowing broader seasonal movements and a more effective military activity (Adams 1977: 383-384; see also Manzo 2004: 81). The recent discovery of Eastern Desert Ware and the cylindrical tumuli typical of the Late Antique phase in the Eastern Desert at Jebel Qoqay/Romeladid, on the southern fringes of the Eastern Desert, may be precisely connected to these movements towards the Eastern Sudan of groups from the north (Manzo *et al.* 2011: 18-27; Manzo 2014d: 241-243). The increased interaction between the Eastern Desert and Eastern Sudan may also be related to the involvement in the management of the trade routes crossing the two regions of groups of the Eastern Desert, made possible by the adoption of camel as a beast of burden (Dijkstra 2012: 246-247; Manzo 2014d: 247).

In this period, the activism of the inhabitants of the deserts, not only of the Beja/Blemmyes of the Eastern Desert, but also of the Noba and Nobatai from the Western Desert, is also related to the crisis of the states in the Nile valley. Not only the Noba penetrated into the middle Nile valley and the Butana, but extended their sphere of action also east of the Atbara, up to the northern fringes of the Aksumite kingdom, where they menaced groups labeled as Barya in the Aksumite inscriptions and this compelled Ezana to launch his well-known in-depth military campaign up to the Nile valley (Hatke 2013: 85-135, 143-147). The few Post-Meroitic sites recorded in Eastern Sudan may well represent this penetration of groups from the west (Manzo 2004: 77; see above 4.3 *The-Post Meroitic sites*). Indeed, from the 4th century AD, after the end of the Kushite power, the contacts between Eastern Sudan and the middle Nile valley started being again evident in the archaeological record and perhaps this somehow represents an indirect confirmation of the inhibitive role previously played by the kingdom of Kush (see above).

As already suggested by these last remarks, starting from the 4th century AD, Eastern Sudan found a new centrality in the new general macro-regional framework: at that time this area on the northern fringes of the Ethio-Eritrean highlands was crossed by the important routes linking the core of the Aksumite kingdom to the Eastern Desert and Egypt, like the one mentioned in the second inscription on the Monumentum Adulitanum, a 3rd century AD text of an Aksumite -or perhaps Adulite- king (Hatke 2013: 59-61). A further factor favoring this new centrality may have been represented, once again, by the raw materials available in the region. Archaeologically, this is perhaps made evident by the occurrence of imported materials arriving from the Mediterranean, perhaps via the Aksumite kingdom, collected on the sites of the Hagiz Group and of the Khatmiya Group, contrasting with their extreme rarity in the contemporaneous sites in the Nile valley south of Lower Nubia (see above 4.1 *The Hagiz Group*, 4.2 *The Khatmiya Group*; see also Manzo 2004: 80).

These remarks, together with recent evidence suggesting the survival of more stable Hagiz Group agricultural communities in the Gash delta (see above 4.1 *The Hagiz Group*), seem also to contradict the traditional view considering 1st millennium AD Eastern Sudan as a backward area, only crossed by nomadic groups. Nevertheless, this makes even more difficult to explain the fact that the southern and very fertile agricultural lands along the Gash and in the Shurab el-Gash area were not more permanently and intensively exploited by Hagiz Group communities. Generally, it should be remarked that the shift of the agro-pastoral economic system to an increasingly mobile nomadic and pastoral model in Eastern Sudan, already evident in the Jebel Mokram Group times and certainly continuing in the 1st millennium BC and 1st millennium AD, cannot be explained on purely environmental bases. This may certainly be connected to a specialized function of the inhabitants of Eastern Sudan and perhaps also of the Eastern Desert in the interaction with the Nile valley and the Ethio-Eritrean highlands. But also factors such as insecurity, especially in the southern agricultural lands, perhaps due to the fledging southern states of the Ethio-Eritrean highlands, as well as other socio-political reasons, remain possible, and the issue certainly requires further investigation.

If from the 3rd to the 6th centuries AD different locally rooted and exogenous groups, presumably interacting among themselves, did cross and inhabit the Eastern Sudan, a similar pattern may have continued in later times, when Christian sites perhaps related to the kingdom of Alwa in the middle Nile valley (see above 4.5 *The Christian sites*) may have coexisted with sites related to the local cultural tradition and perhaps even with the earliest Islamic sites (see above 4.7 *The Islamic sites*). Actually, the increased involvement of the Arabs in the Red Sea trade may have led to a precocious settlement of Arab Muslim merchants on the coast of the Sudan from where they could try to penetrate inland, as well as to trade with the local groups (Fadl Hasan 1967: 63-66, 141-142). This may have led to the establishment of large Islamic graveyards associated with domed tombs along the main routes connecting Eastern Sudan and the Red Sea coast, a tangible demonstration of the penetration and adoption of Islam in the region (Fattovich 2010a: 101-103, 106-107).

Actually, in this period Eastern Sudan may have been a melting pot, not only from a cultural, but also from a religious point of view: traditional and locally rooted beliefs may have met with Christianity and Islam. The occurrence of different funerary structures dating c. AD 1500 (see above 4.6 *The Gergaf Group*, 4.7 *The Islamic sites*) may be related to the variety characterizing the region also from a religious point of view. The fact that some of these funerary structures seem to reflect a typical local taste, but can be very likely ascribed to Islamized groups already using Arabic script (see above 4.6 *The Gergaf Group*), not only throw some light on the possibly long phase of transition to Islam characterizing Eastern Sudan, not surprising also in light of the superficial and sometimes only nominal conversion to Islam of the inhabitants of the region -and of the Eastern Desert- described in several passages by the Arabic sources (Vantini 1975: 153, 161-162, 624, 731), but may also explain how some current peculiar expressions of Islam in this region originated. In this case too, the continuation of the investigations and the elaboration of a fine tuning chronology for this period promises to add further data on these processes.

Chapter 5
Final remarks and perspective of research

Eastern Sudan was already used as a study case in the research on the development of nomadism in ancient northeastern Africa, although admittedly the reasons of the conversion from an agro-pastoral system into an almost fully pastoral one, based on cattle, and later on camel, largely remained unexplained (Sadr 1991: 71, 127-130; and see also above 4.8 *A nomadic melting pot*). Moreover, its participation and relevance in the long-distance exchange network in the 3rd-2nd millennia BC was also demonstrated, and this led to the hypothesis that Eastern Sudan may have been a part of the land of Punt, a region mentioned in the Egyptian texts since the 5th Dynasty, and from where the Egyptians imported African raw materials such as aromatic gums, ebony, ivory, animal skins, and precious metals (Fattovich 1991b, 1991d, 1996; Manzo 1997; and see also above 3.3 *Between Kush and Egypt*). Finally, the importance of Eastern Sudan in the earliest phases of the process of state formation in the northern Horn of Africa, culminated with the development of the kingdom of Aksum, was also suggested (Fattovich 2010b: 150-151, 154-156, 160-162, 167-168). For the rest, the role played by Eastern Sudan in more general dynamics affecting the other regions of northeast Africa largely remained unexplored, and still today a lot remains to be done because the archaeological exploration of the region itself should still be considered in its infancy. Nevertheless, I think that, despite the many unanswered questions and the uncertain points, in the previous chapters it was clearly shown that this role was certainly not marginal. As a matter of fact, there are also reasons to believe that since the earliest phases of its history Eastern Sudan was a crossroads of people, things, and ideas between the middle Nile, the Red Sea, the Eastern Desert and the Ethio-Eritrean highlands, and represented a kind of cultural and eventually ethnic melting pot. Moreover, despite its close ties with the neighboring areas evident in all phases, the region was also precociously characterized by very specific and distinctive traits in its material culture.

Certainly the role of crossroads of the region was facilitated by the environmental setting: resources like pasture and water are not homogeneously distributed through space and even through time, as their availability is affected by a very marked and different seasonal regime (see above 1.3 *The present and past environment*). Despite the environmental changes affecting northeastern Africa in general and in particular our region, this was always true, and most likely always necessitated a certain degree of mobility of the inhabitants of Eastern Sudan and consequently favored the interaction with the neighboring regions. Of course, this was very evident when, with the drier climatic conditions, most likely increasingly affecting Eastern Sudan through the 3rd millennium BC and mainly around 2000 BC (see again 1.3 *The present and past environment*), the quantity of available resources decreased, compelling the human groups living there to extend the area where they could acquire the needed resources. In addition, the presence of so many different ecological niches in the region and in its immediate surroundings, in particular at the foot and along the slopes of the Ethio-Eritrean highlands, represents a further factor which may have also favored the emergence of patterns of repeated seasonal mobility. Nevertheless, it should also be remarked that even after the adoption of livestock, these seasonal movements could not exceed a total of *c.* 400-500km per year, and only after the adoption of the camel the total distance covered in a year by nomadic herders could eventually be longer (Sadr 1987: 280). Therefore, in the case of the contacts over longer distances often involving Eastern Sudan, the possibility of indirect contacts with distant regions involving several groups interacting among them and each one covering just a part of the total distances should be considered, as well as the possibility that climatic changes and environmental crisis sometimes caused actual and permanent migrations of whole groups over longer distances, like it may have perhaps happened at the beginning of the Jebel Mokram Group, a culture characterized by so many ties with the Pan-Grave culture and possibly originating from the arrival of groups from the Eastern Desert (see above 3.4 *In the* aktionsradius *of the Pan-Grave Culture*).

As far as the earliest phases are concerned, given the limited distances separating the Eastern Sudan from the Nile basin, the relationships shown by the material culture with the Nile valley may well be explained by seasonal movements up to the Atbara. Actually, at the very beginning, in the 6th and 5th millennia BC, the east-west relations seem to prevail. At that time Eastern Sudan may have represented the eastern fringes of a broad cultural area centered on the middle Nile valley and extending also west of it, in this specific phase characterized by experiments and experimentations that ultimately led to the adoption of a productive economy. In this general framework, Eastern Sudan may not have been particularly innovative, and may have adopted domesticated animals and plants surprisingly only in the 4th millennium BC, i.e. *c.* 1000 years after the central Nile valley and *c.* 2000 years after Upper Nubia. This may possibly be explained by the proximity of Eastern Sudan to the Ethio-Eritrean highlands that may have mitigated the consequences of the episodes of aridity, that certainly stimulated experimentation and adoption of new subsistence solutions elsewhere. Nevertheless, despite the late adoption of domesticated plants and livestock in our region in the 4th millennium BC, Eastern Sudan may have been crucial in the process of neolithization of northeastern Africa. It may have been precisely thanks to the seasonal movements of pastoral groups of Eastern Sudan towards the Ethio-Eritrean highlands that the spread of domestic cattle and caprovines in those areas took place (see above 2.4 *A broader perspective on Mesolithic and Neolithic: the emerging complexity*). Later on, when the Near Eastern domesticated crops may have shown all their limits in drier climatic conditions, perhaps becoming increasingly evident in our region through the 3rd millennium BC (see above 1.3 *The present and past environment*), the inhabitants of Eastern Sudan may have shown a remarkable attitude in experimentation by extending cultivation to local species -perhaps more fit in the new environmental conditions- like the sorghum (see above 3.1 *The Gash Group*). Interestingly, at that time in Eastern Sudan specific techniques for food preparation such as the cooking of unleavened bread on griddles may have precociously appeared, and were only later adopted on the Ethio-Eritrean highlands for the preparation of *injera* bread from teff (Lyons and D'Andrea 2003), and in the middle Nile valley itself for the preparation of *kisra* bread from sorghum, a cereal which may have been used in that region for a longtime only for making porridge and beer (Edwards 1996: 72).

The African and Near Eastern animal and vegetal domesticated species as well as the favorable ecological conditions of Eastern Sudan may have represented in the 3rd and 2nd millennia BC an economic base on which hierarchic societies may have developed in the region, and this represents a further crucial aspect of its history in those phases. The arising social hierarchy can be possibly already traced in the Butana Group (see above 2.4 *A broader perspective on Mesolithic and Neolithic: the emerging complexity*), it is shown in the Gash Group by the occurrence of administrative devices, by the funerary evidence, and perhaps even by a structured and articulated settlement pattern (see above 3.1 *The Gash Group*), and in the less investigated Jebel Mokram Group by some administrative devices and perhaps again by the settlement pattern (see above 3.2 *The Jebel Mokram Group*). Indeed, like in the case of other regions far from the Mediterranean and the Near Eastern contexts, it should be stressed that this process did not lead to the formation of urban and monumental centers, although the site of Mahal Teglinos (K 1) may have represented a ceremonial center (see above 3.3 *Between Kush and Egypt*). Therefore, Eastern Sudan may well represent a good example of the different models of social complexity deserving to be studied also as a contribution to the more general archaeological and anthropological debate on the concept of complexity (see Chapman 2003: 187-198).

It should be remarked that when the process of sorghum domestication started being evident in the archaeological record, the directionality of the prevailing links involving Eastern Sudan had already changed. Actually, the prevailing east-west relations characterizing the earliest phases, most likely also because of the less intensive occupation of the central Nile valley from the 4th to the 1st millennium BC and of the changing environment, breaking the previous close cultural links across the Sahel (Usai 2016: 19), made room for mostly north-south oriented contacts. In an environmental setting on the way to stabilize, the north-south oriented contacts were certainly favored by the fledging states emerging in the northern part of the Nile valley, in Egypt, in Upper and Lower Nubia, and by their increasing demand for exotic raw materials to be used as rank markers (see e.g. Trigger 1984: 106). From a certain point onwards, the appreciation of some of the raw materials available in Eastern Sudan and nearby (see above 1.4 *The resources*) may have led to the rise of different interactions, particularly related to the exchange of commodities, as perhaps suggested by some finds in the Butana Group, and more clearly evident in Gash Group and Jebel Mokram Group times. These interactions and the relevance of Eastern Sudan in the long-distance exchange network represent a further crucial aspect in the history of the region very evident in the 3rd and 2nd millennia BC, as demonstrated by the abundance of elements suggesting intense contacts with Nubia, the Eastern Desert, the Red Sea and Egypt (see above 3.3 *Between Kush and Egypt*). It should be remarked that for purposes such as the organized trade, longer distances could be systematically covered and this may have been precisely the case of the Egyptian expeditions to the land of Punt characterizing that phase (Fattovich and Bard 2007: 250-253). In turn, this may have increased the involvement of Eastern Sudan -perhaps a part of the land of Punt- in an even broader and busier network. Nevertheless, it is likely that in the meantime the circulation of commodities over long distances may have also continued through more informal patterns of exchange in the framework of the above referred dynamics of seasonal movements characterizing several human groups in the region and around it. Interestingly, the broadening of the network of contacts involving Eastern Sudan to the Red Sea and South Arabia in that phase, together with the rich palaeobotanical evidence the region offers on the process of domestication of the Sahelian crops, and in particular of sorghum (see above and Alemseged Beldados *et al.* nd.a), made of it a crucial area to be studied in the investigation of the spread of African domesticated species to India, via the Red Sea and South Arabia (Fuller and Boivin 2009: 15-16).

The north-south pattern of interactions apparently continued to prevail even in later times, either because the east-west interactions may have been somehow inhibited by the Kushite state in the 1st millennium BC-early 1st millennium AD, and because these relations may have been crucial for the states rooted in the Ethio-Eritrean highlands (see above 4.8 *A nomadic melting pot*). As a result of this, the east-west oriented interactions re-emerged only after the end of the Kushite state, in a phase when the north-south connections with the Eastern Desert and the Ethio-Eritrean highlands continued as well. Moreover, since the end of the 1st millennium AD important, but unfortunately still badly investigated interactions with the Red Sea coast may have favored a possibly precocious adoption of Islam in the region (see again 4.8 *A nomadic melting pot*).

Of course all the above described interactions with neighboring regions and their modality affected the emergence and the development of the regional cultural traditions which are reflected in the material culture. In northeastern Africa, the process of regionalization was often considered as related to the drier climatic conditions characterizing the whole region from the mid-Holocene, that made communication between areas previously sharing several traits in material culture increasingly difficult (see e.g. Keding 1998: 8-9). Nevertheless, the fact that other variables unrelated to environmental conditions are involved in that is made evident by the earliest phase of the cultural sequence of Eastern Sudan: in Pre-Saroba times, despite the still humid conditions, not only regional elements differentiating our region from the Nile valley are already evident, but also evident is a difference at least in the ceramic style between the sites in the northern and the ones in the southern part of the region itself (see above 2.1 *The Pre-Saroba sites and the Amm Adam Group*). To explain this, it may be suggested that the richness in terms of resources of the different ecological niches of Eastern Sudan may have prevented movements and interactions inside the region itself, but this certainly contrasts with the occurrence of shared elements between the southern and the northern groups of Pre-Saroba sites and, in general, between Eastern Sudan and the Nile valley itself (see above 2.4 *A broader perspective on Mesolithic and Neolithic: the emerging complexity*). Of course, a more distinctive original tradition is evident in Eastern Sudan in the

4th millennium BC (see also Marks and Fattovich 1989: 457), also following a pattern known for other regions of ancient Sudan, although some shared traits in the regional ceramic production with the Upper Nubian cultural milieu occur, perhaps to be explained by links originated by the exchange of commodities (see above and 2. 3 *The Butana Group*).

In later phases, intense interactions like the ones recorded for the Gash Group with Nubia, Eastern Desert and even Egypt resulted in a very limited adoption of foreign traits -also from a quantitative point of view- if compared to the later Jebel Mokram Group, when the ceramic production largely overlap in the Pan-Grave one. Also in this case the bigger or more limited openness to the adoption of foreign traits is certainly related to the social context and to the prevailing type of interaction, possibly exchange of commodities for the Gash Group, and repeated seasonal movements or even migration of groups from the Eastern Desert for the Jebel Mokram Group (see above 3.3 *Between Kush and Egypt* and 3.4 *In the* aktionsradius *of the Pan-Grave Culture*).

Later, in the perspective of the origins of the 1st millennium BC ceramic tradition of the Ethio-Eritrean highlands, Eastern Sudan was not only the area through which traits originating in the Nile valley may have passed, but contributed locally rooted traits to the pre-Aksumite pottery, in turn, in the case of the Hagiz Group, also adopting some elements from the pre-Aksumite and Aksumite cultures (see above 4.8 *A nomadic melting pot*). Interestingly, in the 1st millennium AD different groups lived in Eastern Sudan and most likely interacted among them, as suggested e.g. by the occurrence of Khatmiya Group sherds in Hagiz Group assemblages, but despite this, apparently, the material culture of each group largely remained unaffected by the possible adoption of traits of the other groups and kept its distinctiveness and originality (see above 4.8 *A nomadic melting pot*). On the contrary, somehow surprisingly, at that time the different material cultures characterizing some of the groups inhabiting Eastern Sudan were tightly related with the ones of the peoples of the neighboring areas, like the Eastern Desert in the case of the Khatmiya Group, and the middle Nile valley in the case of the Post-Meroitic and Christian sites, perhaps suggesting repeated seasonal movements or even settlement of groups from those regions (see again 4.8 *A nomadic melting pot*). In the meantime, as previously mentioned, the material culture of the Hagiz Group, certainly rooted in the regional tradition, was characterized by traits originating in the Ethio-Eritrean highlands (see again above 4.8 *A nomadic melting pot*).

Clearly, the relevant factors explaining the variety of all these dynamics and their impact on the regional tradition of Eastern Sudan may be related to the way material culture was produced and how this was learned and transmitted, how and with which social meaning material culture was used: all matters related thus to some kind of cultural, social and identity boundaries which may have been expressed, reproduced and also maintained by the material culture (Gosselain 1998: 99-104; see also MacEachern 1998: 129-131). The in-depth investigation of these aspects also through the broadening of their study from ceramics to lithics and to other classes of material culture certainly is a central issue in the agenda of the future research on the development of the regional tradition of Eastern Sudan. In the meantime, this may represent a further relevant contribution the continuation of investigation on this crucial region may potentially offer to the more general historical and anthropological debate.

References

Abdalla, A.M. 1989. Meroitic Kush, Abyssinia and Arabia. A contribution to the Hauptreferat: L. Török, Kush and the external world. In S. Donadoni and S. Wenig (eds.), *Studia Meroitica 1984*: 383-387. Berlin, Akademie Verlag (*Meroitica* 10).

Adams, W.Y. 1977. *Nubia. Corridor to Africa*. London, Allen Lane.

Alemseged Beldados 2015. *Paleoethnobotanical Study of Ancient Food Crops and the Environmental Context in North-East Africa, 6000 BC-AD 200/300*. Oxford, Archaeopress (*Cambridge Monographs in African Archaeology* 88, British Archaeological Reports International Series 2706).

Alemseged Beldados and Costantini, L. 2011. Sorghum Exploitation at Kassala and Its Environs, North Eastern Sudan in the Second and First Millennia BC. *Nyame Akuma* 75: 33-39.

Alemseged Beldados, Manzo, A., Murphy, C., Stevens, C.J., and Fuller, D.Q. nd.a. Evidence of sorghum cultivation and introduced West Africa crops in the Second Millennium BCE at Kassala, Eastern Sudan. In A.M. Mercuri, A.C. D'Andrea, R. Fornaciari and A. Höhn (eds.), *Plants and People in the African Past: Progress in African Archaeobotany*, in press.

Anderson, J.R. and Welsby, D.A. (eds.) 2014. *The Fourth Cataract and Beyond. Proceedings of the 12th International Conference for Nubian Studies*. Leuven-Paris-Walpole, Peeters (*British Museum Publications on Egypt and Sudan* 1).

Arkell, A.J. 1954. Four Occupation Sites at Agordat. *Kush* 2: 33-62.

Aston, B.G, Harrell, J.A. and Shaw, I. 2000. Stone. In Nicholson and Shaw (eds.) 2000: 5-77

Bard, K.A., Fattovich, R. 2007. Synthesis. In K.A. Bard and R. Fattovich (eds.), *Harbor of the Pharaohs to the Land of Punt. Archaeological Investigations at Mersa/Wadi Gawasis, Egypt, 2001-2005*: 239-253. Naples, Il Torcoliere, Università degli Studi di Napoli 'L'Orientale'.

Barbour, K.M. 1961. *The Republic of the Sudan. A Regional Geography*. London, London University Press.

Barnard, H. 2012. Introduction to Part I. From Adam to Alexander (500.000-2500 Years Ago). In Barnard and Duistermaat (eds.) 2012: 2-23.

Barnard, H. and Duistermaat, K. (eds.) 2012. *The History of the Peoples of the Eastern Desert*. Los Angeles, Cotsen Institute of Archaeology Press (*Cotsen Institute of Archaeology Monograph* 73).

Bietak, M. 1966. *Ausgrabungen in Sayala-Nubien 1961-1965: Denkmäler der C-Gruppe und der Pan-Gräber-Kultur*. Wien, Verlag der Österreichischen Akademie der Wissenschaften (*Akademie der Wissenschaften in Wien, Phil.-Hist. Klasse, Denkschrift* 92).

Bietak, M. 1968. *Studien zur Chronologie der Nubischen C-Gruppe Kultur. Ein Beitrag zur Frügeschichte Unternubiens zwischen 2200 und 1550 vor Chr.*, Wien, Verlag der Österreichischen Akademie der Wissenschaften (*Akademie der Wissenschaften in Wien, Phil.-Hist. Klasse, Denkschrift* 97).

Bintliff, J.L. and Barnard, H. 2012. Concluding Remarks. In Barnard and Duistermaat (eds.) 2012: 429-444.

Bonnet, C. 1997. Kerma: rapport préliminaire sur les campagnes de 1995-1996 et 1996-1997. *Genava* n.s. 45: 96-112.

Bonnet, C. 2013. Découverte d'une nouvelle ville cérémonielle nubienne et le *menenou* de Thoutmosis Ier (Doukki Gel, Soudan). *Académie des Inscriptions et Belles-Lettres. Comptes Rendus*, avril-juin: 807-823.

Bonnet, C. 2014. Forty Years Research on Kerma Cultures. In Anderson and Welsby (eds.) 2014: 81-93.

Bonnet, C. and Reinold, J. 1993. Deux rapports de prospection dans le désert oriental. Genava n.s. 41: 19-26.

Booth, A. 1952. The forests in Upper Nile Province, 1862-1950. *Sudan Notes & Records* 34: 113-243.

Bradley, R. 1992. *Nomads in the Archaeological Record. Case Studies in the Northern Provinces of the Sudan*. Berlin, Akademie Verlag (*Meroitica* 13).

Brandt, S.A., Manzo, A. and Perlignieri, C. 2008. Linking the Highlands and Lowlands: Implications of a Test Excavation at Kokan Rockshelter, Agordat, Eritrea. In P.R. Schmidt, M.C. Curtis and Zelalem Tekla (eds.), *The Archaeology of Ancient Eritrea*: 33-48. Trenton, Red Sea Press.

Brass, M.J. 2014. Interactions and Pastoralism Along the Southern and Southeastern Frontiers of the Meroitic State, Sudan. *Journal of World Prehistory* 28: 255-288.

Brass, M.J. 2016. *Reinterpreting chronology and society at the mortuary complex of Jebel Moya (Sudan)*. Oxford, Archaeopress (*Cambridge Monographs in African Archaeology* 92).

Bubenzer, O., Bolten, A. and Darius, F. (eds.) 2007. Atlas of cultural and environmental change in Arid Africa, Köln, Heinrich-Barth-Institut (*Africa Praehistorica* 21).

Callow, G. and Kabir, A.M. 2003. Erkowit, a Neolithic Site in the Red Sea Hills (Sudan): interim report on the pottery. *Sudan & Nubia* 7: 62-65.

Caneva, I. 1996. The influence of Saharan prehistoric cultures on the Nile Valley. In G. Aumassip, J. D. Clark and F. Mori (eds.), *The prehistory of Africa*: 231–239. Forlì, A.B.A.C.O.

Capuano, G., Manzo, A. and Perlingieri, C.1994. Progress Report on the Pottery from the Gash Group Settlement at Mahal Teglinos (Kassala), 3rd-2nd mill. BC. In C. Bonnet (ed.), *Études Nubiennes. Conférence de Genève, Actes du VIIe Congrès international d'études nubiennes 3-8 septembre 1990*, Vol. II: 109-115. Genève, Mission Archéologique de l'Université de Genève au Soudan.

Chapman, R. 2003. *Archaeologies of Complexity*. London and New York, Routledge.

Close, A. E. 2002. Sinai, Sahara, Sahel: The introduction of domestic caprines to Africa. In T. Lenssen-Erz, U. Tegtmeier, S. Kröpelin *et al.* (eds.), *Tides of the desert—Gezeiten der Wüste. Contributions to the archaeology and environmental history of Africa in honour of Rudolph Kuper*: 471–483. Köln, Heinrich-Barth-Institut (*Africa Praehistorica* 14).

Conti Rossini, C. 1903. Documenti per l'archeologia eritrea nella bassa valle del Barca. *Rendiconti della Reale Accademia dei* Lincei 12: 139-147.

Corbet, G.B. 1978. *The Mammals of the Palaearctic Region*. London and Ithaca, British Museum of Natural History and Cornell University Press.

Costantini, L., Fattovich, R., Pardini, E., and Piperno, M. 1982. Preliminary Report of Archaeological Investigations at Mahal Teglinos (Kassala) November 1981. *Nyame Akuma* 21: 30-33.

Costantini, L., Fattovich, R., Piperno, M. and Sadr, K. 1983. Gash Delta Archaeological Project: 1982 field season. *Nyame Akuma* 23: 17-19.

Cremaschi, M., D'Alessandro, A., Fattovich, R. and Piperno, M. 1986. Gash Delta Archaeological Project: 1985 Field Season. *Nyame Akuma* 27: 45-48.

Crowfoot, J.W. 1922. A Note on the Date of the Towers. *Sudan Notes and Records* 5: 83-87.

Crowfoot, J.W. 1928. Some Potsherds from Kassala. *Journal of Egyptian Archaeology* 14: 112-116.

Cumming, D.C. 1937. The History of Kassala and the Province of Taka. *Sudan Notes & Records* 20: 1-45.

D'Andrea, C.A. and Tsubakisaka, Y. 1990. Plant Remains Preserved in Kassala Phase Ceramics, Eastern Sudan. *Nyame Akuma* 33: 16.

Dardano, A. and Riccardi, R. 1936. *Atlante d'Africa*. Milano, Ulrico Hoepli.

Davies, V.W. 2003. Kush in Egypt: a new historical inscription. *Sudan & Nubia* 7: 52-54.

Davies, V.W. 2014. The Korosko Road Project. Recording Egyptian inscriptions in the Eastern Desert and elsewhere. *Sudan & Nubia* 18: 30-44.

De Souza, A. 2013. The Egyptianisation of the Pan-Grave Culture: a new look at an old idea. *The Bulletin of the Australian Centre for Egyptology* 24: 109-126.

Dijkstra, J. H. F. 2012. Blemmyes, Noubades and the Eastern Desert in Late Antiquity. Reassessing the Written Sources. In Barnard and Duistermaat (eds.) 2012: 239-247

Edwards, D.N. 1989. *Archaeology and settlement in Upper Nubia in the 1st Millennium AD*, Oxford, (*Cambridge Monographs in African Archaeology* 36, *British Archaeological Reports International Series* 537).

Edwards, D.N. 1996. Sorghum, Beer and Kushite Society. *Norwegian Archaeological Review* 29: 65-77.

Edwards, D.N. and Osman, A. (with contributions by Y. Fadl Tahir, I. Soghayroun el-Zein, A. Sadis and others) 1989. *The Archaeology of a Nubian Frontier. Survey of the Nile Third Cataract, Sudan*. Leicester, Mauhaus.

Elsadig, S.O. 2000. The Domed Tombs of the Eastern Sudan. *Sudan & Nubia* 4: 37-43.

Emberling, G. and Williams, B.B. 2010. The Kingdom of Kush in the 4th Cataract: Archaeological Salvage of the Oriental Institute Nubian Expedition 2007 season (part I). Preliminary report on the sites of Hosh el-Guruf and El-Widay. *Gdańsk Archaeological Museum and Heritage Protection Fund African Reports* 7: 7-38.

Emberling, G., Williams, B.B., Ingvoldstad, M. and James, T.R. 2014. Peripheral Vision: Identity at the Margins of the Early Kingdom of Kush. In Anderson and Welsby (eds.) 2014: 329-336.

Espinel, A.D. 2011. *Abriendo los caminos de Punt. Contactos entre Egipto y el ambiente afroárabe dunate la Edad del Bronce [ca. 3000 a.C.-1065 a.C.]*. Barcelona, Bellaterra.

Fadl Hasan, Y. 1967. *The Arabs of the Sudan*. Edinburgh, Edinburgh University Press.

Fattovich, R. 1982. The Problem of Sudanese-Ethiopian Contacts in Antiquity: Status Quaestionis and Current Trends of Research. In J.M. Plumley (ed.), *Nubian Studies. Proceedings of the Symposium for Nubian Studies*: 76-86. Warminster, Aris & Phillips.

Fattovich, R. 1989a. The late prehistory of the Gash Delta (Eastern Sudan). In L. Krzyżaniak and M. Kobusiewicz (eds.), *Late Prehistory of the Nile Basin and the Sahara*: 481-498. Poznań, Muzeum Archeologiczne w Poznaniu (*Studies in African Archaeology* 2).

Fattovich, R. 1989b. Il sito protostorico di Mahal Teglinos presso Kassala (Sudan Orientale). *Rivista di Antropologia* 67: 221-238.

Fattovich, R.1989c. The Stelae of Kassala: A New Type of Funerary Monument in the Eastern Sudan. *Archéologie du Nil Moyen* 3: 55-69.

Fattovich, R. 1989d. The Gash Delta between 1000 BC and AD 1000. In S. Donadoni and S. Wenig (eds.), *Studia Meroitica 1984*: 797-816. Berlin, Akademie Verlag (*Meroitica* 10).

Fattovich, R. 1990a. The Peopling of the Northern Ethiopian-Sudanese Borderland between 7000 and 1000 BP: A Preliminary Model. *Nubica* I/II: 3-45.

Fattovich, R. 1990b. Gash Delta Archaeological Project: 1988-89 Field Season. *Nyame Akuma* 33: 16-20.

Fattovich, R. 1991a. Ricerche archeologiche italiane nel delta del Gash (Kassala), 1980-1989, un bilancio preliminare. *Rassegna di Studi Etiopici* 33 [1989]: 89-130.

Fattovich, R. 1991b. At the Periphery of the Empire: The Gash Delta (Eastern Sudan). In V.W. Davies (ed.), *Egypt and Africa. Nubia from Prehistory to Islam*: 40-48. London: The British Museum Press.

Fattovich, R. 1991c. Evidence of Possible Administrative Devices in the Gash Delta (Kassala), 3rd-2nd millennia BC. *Archéologie du Nil Moyen* 5: 65-78.

Fattovich, R. 1991d. The problem of Punt in the light of recent field work in the Eastern Sudan. In S. Schoske (ed.), *Akten des vierten Internationalen Aegyptologen Kongresses-München 1985. Band 4. Geschichte-Werwaltung- und Wirtschaftgestichte-Rechtgeschichte-Nachbarkulturen*: 257-272. Hamburg, Buske.

Fattovich, R. 1993a. Excavations at Mahal Teglinos (Kassala), 1984-1988. A Preliminary Report. *Kush* 16: 225-287.

Fattovich, R. 1993b. The Gash Group of the Eastern Sudan: an outline. In L. Krzyżaniak, M. Kobusiewicz and J. Alexander (eds.), *Environmental Change and Human Culture in the Nile Basin and the Northern Africa until the Second Millennium BC*: 439-448. Poznań, Muzeum Archeologiczne w Poznaniu (*Studies in African Archaeology* 4).

Fattovich, R. 1994. Sulle origini dei Baria e dei Cunama. In Yaqob Beyene, R. Fattovich, P. Marrassini and A. Triulzi (eds.), *Etiopia e Oltre. Studi in onore di Lanfranco Ricci*: 27-67. Naples, Istituto Universitario Orientale (*Istituto Universitario Orientale, Studi Africanistici, Serie Etiopica* 1).

Fattovich, R. 1995. The Gash Group. A Complex Society in the lowlands to the East of the Nile. In *Actes de la VIIIe Conférence Internationale des Etudes Nubiennes*, vol. I: 191-200. Villeneuve-d'Ascq, Université Charles-de-Gaulle-Lille III (*Cahiers de Recherches de l'Institut de Papyrologie et d'Egyptologie de Lille* 17/1).

Fattovich, R. 1996. Punt: The Archaeological Perspective. *Beiträge zur Sudanforschung* 6: 15-29.

Fattovich, R. 2006-2007. Aqiq: a coastal site in the Red Sea, Sudan. In B. Gratien (ed.), *Mélanges offerts à Francis Geus* : 87-97. Villeneuve-d'Ascq, Université Charles-de-Gaulle-Lille III (*Cahiers de Recherches de l'Institut de Papyrologie et d'Egyptologie de Lille* 26).

Fattovich, R. 2010a. The Early Spread of Islam in the Eritrean-Sudanese Lowlands (ca. AD 800-1500) from an Archaeological Perspective. In A. Gori and B. Scarcia Amoretti (eds.), *L'Islam in Etiopia. Bilanci e prospettive*: 89-107. Rome, Edizioni di Storia e Letteratura (*Civiltà del Mediterraneo* 16-17).

Fattovich, R. 2010b. The Development of Ancient States in the Northern Horn of Africa, c. 3000 BC–AD 1000: An Archaeological Outline. *Journal of World Prehistory* 23: 145-175.

Fattovich, R., Manzo, A. and Usai, D. 1994. Gash Delta Archaeological Project: 1991, 1992-93, 1993-94 field seasons. *Nyame Akuma* 42: 14-18.

Fattovich, R., Marks, A.E. and Mohammed Ali, A. 1984. The archaeology of the Eastern Sahel, Sudan: preliminary results. *African Archaeological Review* 2: 173-188.

Fattovich, R., Sadr, K. and Vitagliano, S. 1988-1989. Society and Territory in the Gash Delta (Kassala, Eastern Sudan) 3000 BC-AD 300/400. *Origini* 14: 329-358.

Fattovich, R. and Vitagliano, S. 1987. Gash Delta Archaeological Project: 1987 Field Season. *Nyame Akuma* 29: 56-59.

Friedman, R. 2002. Foreword. In R. Friedman (ed.) 2002: xiii-xv.

Friedman, R. (ed.) 2002. *Egypt and Nubia. Gifts of the Deserts*, London, The British Museum Press.

Fuller, D.Q. and Boivin, N. 2009. Crops, Cattle and Commensals across the Indian Ocean: Current and Potential Archaeobiological Evidence. *Études Océan Indien* 42-43: 13-46.

Gale, R., Gasson, P., Hepper, N. and Killen, G. 2000. Wood. In Nicholson and Shaw (eds.) 2000: 334-371.

Gautier, A. and Van Neer, W. 2006. Animal Remains from Mahal Teglinos (Kassala, Sudan) and the Arrival of Pastoralism in the Southern Atbai. *Journal of African Archaeology* 4: 223-233.

Geraads, D. 1983. Faunal Remains from the Gash Delta, Sudan. *Nyame Akuma* 23: 2.

Giuliani, S. 2004. Some Cultural Aspects of the *Medja* of the Eastern Desert. In T. Kendall (ed.), *Nubian Studies 1998. Proceedings of the Ninth Conference of the International Society of Nubian Studies*: 286-290. Boston, Northeastern University (Boston, Mass.), Department of African-American Studies.

Gosselain, O.P. 1998. Social and Technical Identity in a Clay Crystal Ball. In M.T. Stark (ed.), *The Archaeology of Social Boundaries*: 78-106. Washington and London, Smithsonian Institute Press.

Grasse, P.P. 1955. *Traité de Zoologie, Anatomie, Systématique, Biologie*, Vol. 17. Paris, Masson.

Gratien, B. 1978. *Les cultures Kerma. Essai de classification*. Villeneuve-d'Ascq, Publications de l'Université de Lille III.

Haaland, R. 2014. The Meroitic Empire: trade and Cultural Influences in an Indian Ocean Context. *African Archaeological Review* 31: 649–673.

Hardy-Smith, T. and Edwards, P. C. 2004. The Garbage Crisis in prehistory: Artefact discard patterns at the Early Natufian site of Wadi Hammeh 27 and the origins of household refuse disposal strategies. *Journal of Anthropological Archaeology* 23: 253–289.

Hassan, F.A. 2002. Palaeclimate, Food and Culture Change in Africa: an Overview. In F.A. Hassan (ed.), *Droughts, Food & Culture: Ecological Change & Food Security in Africa's Later Prehistory*: 11-26. New York, Kluwer Academic/Plenum Publishers.

Hatke, G. 2013. Aksum and Nubia. *Warfare, Commerce, and Political Fictions in Ancient Northeast Africa*. New York, New York University Press, Institute for the Study of the Ancient World.

Hepper, F.N. 1969. Arabian and African Frankincense Trees. *Journal of Egyptian Archaeology* 55: 66-72.

Hinkel, M.1994. The Water Reservoirs in Ancient Sudan. In C. Bonnet (ed.), *Etudes nubiennes. Conférence de Genève. Actes du VIIe Congrès International d'études nubiennes*. Volume II. Communications: 171-175. Genève, Mission Archéologique de l'Université de Genève au Soudan.

Honegger, M. 2004. Settlements and cemeteries of the Mesolithic and Early Neolithic at el-Barga (Kerma region). *Sudan & Nubia* 8: 27-32.

Honegger, M. 2014a. Recent Advances in Our Understanding of Prehistory in Northern Sudan. In Anderson and Welsby (eds.) 2014: 19-30.

Honegger, M. 2014b. *Aux origines des pharaons noirs. 10000 ans d'archéologie en Nubie*, Neuchâtel, Editions du Laténium.

Hurst, H.E. 1952. *The Nile*. London, Constable.

James, H. 1867. *Routes in Abyssinia*. Simla, unspecified publishing company.

Jesse, F., Kröpelin, S., Lange, M., Pöllath, N. and Berke, H. 2004. On the Periphery of Kerma – the Handessi Horizon in the Wadi Hariq, Northwestern Sudan. *Journal of African Archaeology* 2: 123-164.

Keding, B. 1998. The Yellow Nile: new data on settlement and the environment in the Sudanese Eastern Sahara. *Sudan & Nubia* 2: 2-12.

Keding, B. 2004. The Yellow Nile: Settlement Shifts in the Wadi Howar Region (Sudanese Eastern Sahara) and Adjacent Areas from between the Sixth to the First Millennium BC. In T. Kendall (ed.), *Nubian Studies 1998. Proceedings of the Ninth Conference of the International Society of Nubian Studies*: 95-108. Boston, Northeastern University (Boston, Mass.), Department of African-American Studies.

Klemm, R. and Klemm, D. 2013. *Gold and Gold Mining in Ancient Egypt and Nubia. Geoarchaeology of the Ancient Gold Mining Sites in the Egyptian and Sudanese Eastern Desert.* Heidelberg, Dordrecht, New York and London, Springer (Natural Science in Archaeology).

Krzyszkowska, O. and Morkot, R. 2000. Ivory and related materials. In Nicholson and Shaw (eds.) 2000: 320-331.

Kuper, R. 2002. Routes and Roots in Egypt's Western Desert. The Early Holocene Resettlement of the Eastern Sahara. In R. Friedman (ed.) 2002: 1-12.

Kuper, R. and Kröpelin, S. 2006. Climate-Controlled Holocene Occupation in the Sahara: Motor of Africa's Evolution. *Science* 313: 803-807.

Lesur, J., Hildebrand, E.A., Abawa, G., Gutherz, X. 2013. The advent of herding in the Horn of Africa: New data from Ethiopia, Djibouti and Somaliland. *Quaternary International* 343: 148-158.

Lyons, D. and D'Andrea, C.A. 2003. Griddles, Ovens, and Agricultural Origins: An Ethnoarchaeological Study of Bread Baking in Highland Ethiopia. *American Anthropologist* 105: 515-530.

MacEachern, S. 1998. Scale, Style, and Cultural Variations. Technological Traditions in Northern Mandara Mountains. In M.T. Stark (ed.), *The Archaeology of Social Boundaries*: 107-131. Washington and London, Smithsonian Institute Press.

Mackworth-Praed, C.W. and Grant, C.H.B. 1981. *African Handbook of Birds, Eastern and North Africa.* London and New York, Longmans.

Manetti, C. 1936. *Etiopia economica.* Panorama economico agrario dell'Africa Orientale Italiana e dell'Abissinia. Firenze, Bemporad & F.

Manzo, A. 1993. Note sur quelques tessons égyptiens découverts près de Kassala (Sud-Est du Soudan). *Bulletin de Liaison du Groupe International d'Étude de la céramique égyptienne* 17: 41-44.

Manzo, A. 1996. *Culture ed ambiente: l'Africa nord-orientale nei dati archeologici e nelle fonti letterarie ellenistiche.* Naples, Istituto Universitario Orientale (Supplemento agli Annali dell'Istituto Universitario Orientale 87).

Manzo, A. 1997. Les tessons 'exotiques' du Groupe du Gash: un essai d'examen statistique. In *Actes de la VIIIe Conférence Internationale des Etudes Nubiennes*, vol. II : 77-87. Villeneuve-d'Ascq, Université Charles-de-Gaulle-Lille III (Cahiers de Recherches de l'Institut de Papyrologie et d'Egyptologie de Lille 17/2).

Manzo, A. 1998. The Dynamics of External Contacts of Northern Ethiopia and Eritrea from Proto-Historical to Askumite Times, Late 2nd Millennium BC-Late 1st Millennium AD. In *3. Wissenschaftliche Tagung des Orbis Aethiopicus. Äthiopien und seine Nachbarn/Ethiopia and its Neighbours*: 35-52. Gdánsk and Frankfurt, Muzeum Archeologiczne and Orbis Aethiopicus.

Manzo, A. 1999. *Echanges et contacts le long du Nil et de la Mer Rouge à l'époque protohistorique (IIIe et IIe millénaire avant J.-C.). Une synthèse préliminaire.* Oxford, Archaeopress (Cambridge Monographs in African Archaeology 48, British Archaeological Reports International Series 782).

Manzo, A. 2007. Tokens, pottery disks, and other administrative devices: two case studies between Nubia and Ethiopia. In A.M. D'Onofrio (ed.), *Tallies, Tokens & Counters. From the Mediterranean to India*: 51-61. Naples, Il Torcoliere, Università degli Studi di Napoli 'L'Orientale'.

Manzo, A. 2012. From the sea to the deserts and back: New research in Eastern Sudan. *British Museum Studies in Ancient Egypt and Sudan* 18: 75-106.

Manzo, A. 2013. The Italian Archaeological Expedition to the Eastern Sudan of the Università degli Studi di Napoli 'L'Orientale'. An Overview of the 2012 field season. *Newsletter di Archeologia CISA* 4: 253-271.

Manzo, A. 2014a. Preliminary Report of the 2013 Field Season of the Italian Archaeological Expedition to the Eastern Sudan of the Università degli Studi di Napoli 'L'Orientale'. *Newsletter di Archeologia CISA* 5: 375-412.

Manzo, A. 2014b. Beyond the Fourth Cataract. Perspectives for Research in Eastern Sudan. In Anderson and Welsby (eds.) 2014: 1149-1157.

Manzo, A. 2014c. *Snakes and Sacrifices: Tentative Insights into the Pre-Christian Ethiopian Religion.* Æthiopica 17: 7-24.

Manzo, A. 2014d. New Eastern Desert Ware Finds from Sudan and Ethiopia. In A. Lohwasser and P. Wolf (eds.), *Ein Forscherleben zwischen den Welten. Zum 80. Geburtstag von Steffen Wenig*: 237-252. Berlin, Sudanarchäologische Gesellschaft zu Berlin (*Der antike Sudan. Mitteilungen der Sudanarchäologische Gesellschaft zu Berlin e. V.*)

Manzo, A. 2015. Italian Archaeological Expedition to the Eastern Sudan of the Università degli studi di Napoli 'L'Orientale'. Preliminary Report of the 2014 Field Season. *Newsletter di Archeologia CISA* 6: 231-240.

Manzo, A. 2016. Italian Archaeological Expedition to the Eastern Sudan of the University of Naples 'L'Orientale'. Preliminary Report of the 2015 Field Season. *Newsletter di Archeologia CISA* 7: 191-202.

Manzo, A. nd.a. The Chronology of the Transition between the Gash Group and the Jebel Mokram Group of Eastern Sudan (2nd millennium BC). In M. Honneger (ed.) *Proceedings of the 13th International Conference of the Society for Nubian Studies*, in press.

Manzo, A. nd.b. Egyptian ceramics from Eastern Sudan (Kassala region). In R. David (ed.), *Céramiques égyptiennes au Soudan: importations, imitations et influences*. Cairo, Institut Français d'Archéologie Orientale (*Cahiers de la Céramique Égyptienne* 12), in press.

Manzo, A. (with contributions by A. Coppa, Alemseged Beldados, and V. Zoppi) 2011. *Italian Archaeological Expedition to the Sudan of the University of Naples 'L'Orientale'. 2010 Field Season*. Naples, Il Torcoliere, Università degli Studi di Napoli 'L'Orientale'.

Manzo, A. (with contributions by Alemseged Beldados, A. Carannante, D. Usai and V. Zoppi) 2012. *Italian Archaeological Expedition to the Sudan of the University of Naples 'L'Orientale'. 2011 Field Season*. Naples, Il Torcoliere, Università degli Studi di Napoli 'L'Orientale'.

Marks, A.E. 1987. Terminal Pleistocene and Holocene Hunters and Gatherers in the Eastern Sudan. *African Archaeological Review* 5: 79-92.

Marks, A.E. and Fattovich, R. 1989. The later prehistory of the Eastern Sudan: a preliminary view. In L. Krzyżaniak and M. Kobusiewicz (eds.), *Late Prehistory of the Nile Valley and the Sahara*: 451-458. Poznań, Muzeum Archeologiczne w Poznaniu (*Studies in African Archaeology* 2).

Marks, A.E. and Mohammed Ali, A. 1980. Survey of Northern Butana. *Nyame Akuma* 16: 30-35.

Marks, A.E. and Sadr, K. 1988. Holocene Environments and Occupations in the Southern Atbai, Sudan: A Preliminary Formulation. In J. Bower and D. Lubell (eds.), *Prehistoric Cultures and Environments in the Late Quaternary of Africa*: 69-90. Oxford: British Archaeological Reports (*British Archaeological Reports International Series* 405, *Cambridge Monographs in African Archaeology* 26).

Maydon, H.C. 1924. Across Eritrea. *Geographical Journal* 63: 45-56.

Mohammed Ahmed, S. 1997. More than a Century of Archaeological Research in the Sudan. In D. Wildung (ed.), *Sudan. Ancient Kingdoms of the Nile*: 1-5. Paris-New York, Flammarion.

Monneret de Villard, U. 1938. Note sulle influenze asiatiche nell'Africa orientale. *Rivista degli Studi Orientali* 17: 303-349.

Morrice, H.A. 1949. The Development of Sudan Communications. *Sudan Notes & Records* 30: 1-38, 141-178.

Munzinger, W. 1890. *Studi sull'Africa Orientale*. Roma, Voghera Carlo.

Näsr, C. 2012. Nomads at the Nile: Towards and Archaeology of Interaction. In Barnard and Duistermaat (eds.) 2012: 81-89.

Nicholson, P.T. and Shaw, I. (eds.) 2000. *Ancient Egyptian Materials and Technology*. Cambridge, Cambridge University Press.

Nicoll, K. 2001. Radiocarbon chronologies for prehistoric human occupation and hydroclimatic change in Egypt and Northern Sudan. *Geoarchaeology: An International Journal* 16 (1): 47–64.

Nicoll, K. 2004. Recent environmental change and prehistoric human activity in Egypt and Northern Sudan. *Quaternary Science Reviews* 23: 561–580.

Obsomer, C. 2007. L'empire nubien des Sésostris: Ouaouat et Kouch sous la XIIe dynastie. In M.-C. Bruwier (ed.), *Pharaons noirs sur la piste des quarante jours*: 53-75. Mariemont, Musée Royal de Mariemont.

Ogden, J. 2000. Metals. In Nicholson and Shaw (eds.) 2000: 148-176.

Osborn, D.J. and Osbornová, J. 1998. *The Mammals of Ancient Egypt*. Warminster, Aris & Phillips.

Paner, E. 2014. Kerma Culture in the Fourth Cataract of the Nile. In Anderson and Welsby (eds.) 2014: 53-79.

Paul, A. 1952. Ancient Tombs in Kassala Province. *Sudan Notes and Records* 33: 54-57.

Peters, J. 1989. Faunal Remains and Environmental Change in Central and Eastern Sudan from Terminal Pleistocene to Middle Holocene Times. *Academiae Analecta* 51: 123-148.

Peters, J. 1992. Late Quaternary Mammalian Remains from Central and Eastern Sudan and their Palaeoenvironmental Significance. *Palaeoecology of Africa* 23: 91-115.

Phillips, J. 2000. Ostrich eggshells. In Nicholson and Shaw (eds.) 2000, 332-333.

Phillips, J. 2014. The Foreign Contacts of Ancient Aksum: New finds and some random thoughts. In A. Lohwasser and P. Wolf (eds.), *Ein Forscherleben zwischen den Welten. Zum 80. Geburtstag von Steffen Wenig*: 253-268. Berlin, Sudanarchäologische Gesellschaft zu Berlin (*Der antike Sudan. Mitteilungen der Sudanarchäologische Gesellschaft zu Berlin e. V.*).

Privati, B. 1990. Les ateliers de potiers et leur production. In C. Bonnet (ed.), *Kerma, royaume de Nubie*: 121-13. Genève, Mission Archéologique de l'Université de Genève au Soudan.

Reisner, G.A. 1923, *Excavations at Kerma*, Parts IV-V. Cambridge Mass., Peabody Museum of Harvard University (*Harvard African Studies* 6).

Sadr, K. 1984. The Gergaf Group. *Nyame Akuma*: 24-25: 33-35.

Sadr, K. 1987. The Territorial Expanse of the Pan-Grave Culture. *Archéologie du Nil Moyen* 2: 265-291.

Sadr, K. 1988. Settlement Patterns and Land Use in the Late Prehistoric Southern Atbai, East Central Sudan. *Journal of Field Archaeology* 15: 381-401.

Sadr, K. 1990. The Medjay in Southern Atbai. *Archéologie du Nil Moyen* 4: 63-86.

Sadr, K. 1991. *The Development of Nomadism in Ancient Northeast Africa*. Philadelphia, University of Pennsylvania Press.

Sadr, K., Castiglioni, A. and Castiglioni, A. 1995. Nubian Desert Archaeology: a Preliminary View. *Archéologie du Nil Moyen* 7: 203-235.

Salvatori, S. 2012. Disclosing Archaeological Complexity of the Khartoum Mesolithic: New Data at the Site and Regional Level. *African Archaeological Review* 29: 399-472.

Salvatori, S. and Usai, D. (eds.) 2008. *A Neolithic Cemetery in the Northern Dongola Reach. Excavations at Site R12*. Oxford, Archaeopress (*Sudan Archaeological Research Society Publication* 16, British Archaeological Reports 1814).

Salvatori, S., Usai, D. and Zerboni, A. 2011. Mesolithic Site Formation and Palaeoenvironment Along the White Nile (Central Sudan). *African Archaeological Review* 28: 177-211.

Säve-Söderbergh, T. 1941. *Ägypten und Nubien. Ein Beitrag zur Geschichte altägyptischer Aussenpolitik*. Lund, Håkan Ohlssons Boktryckeri.

Scaweinfurth, G. 1891. Le piante utili dell'Eritrea. *Bollettino della Società Africana d'Italia* 10: 233-286.

Serpico, M. 2000. Resins, amber and bitumen. In Nicholson and Shaw (eds.) 2000: 430-474.

Shaw, I. (ed.) 2000. *The Oxford History of Ancient Egypt*. Oxford, Oxford University Press.

Shiner, J.L. (with the contribution of A. Marks, V. Chmielewski, J. de Heinzelin and T.R. Hays) 1971. *The Prehistory and Geology of Northern Sudan. Part II*. Dallas, unpublished report to the National Science Foundation, Grant GS 1192.

Smither, P.C. 1945. The Semnah Despatches. *Journal of Egyptian Archaeology* 31: 3-10.

Thompson, D.E. 1976. Languages of Northern Eritrea. In M.L. Bender (ed.), *The Non-Semitic Languages of Ethiopia*: 597-603. East Lansing, African Studies Center, Michigan State University (*Committee on Ethiopian Studies Occasional Papers Series Monograph* 5).

Török, L. 2009. *Between Two Worlds. The Frontier Region between Ancient Nubia and Egypt 3700 BC-AD 500*. Leiden-Boston, Brill (*Probleme der Ägyptologie* 29).

Trigger, B.G. 1965. *History and Settlement in Lower Nubia*. New Haven, Yale University, Department of Anthropology (*Yale University Publications in Anthropology* 69).

Trigger, B.G. 1984. The mainlines of socio-economic development in dynastic Egypt to the end of the Old Kingdom. In L. Krzyżaniak and M. Kobusiewicz (eds.), *Origin and Early Development of Food-producing Cultures in North-eastern Africa*: 101-108. Poznań, Muzeum Archeologiczne w Poznaniu (*Studies in African Archaeology* 1).

Trigger, B.G. 1994. Paradigms in Sudan Archaeology. *The International Journal of African Historical Studies* 27: 323-345.

Tyson Smith S. 2003. *Wretched Kush: ethnic identities and boundaries in Egypt's Nubian empire*. London, Routledge.

Usai, D. 1997. Preliminary analysis of Mahal Teglinos lithic industry. In *Actes de la VIIIe Conference Internationale des Etudes Nubiennes*, II: 89-97. Lille, Villeneuve-d'Ascq, Université Charles-de-Gaulle-Lille III (*Cahiers de Recherches de l'Institut de Papyrologie et d'Egyptologie de Lille* 17/2).

Usai, D. 2002. Work in progress: the Gash Group lithic industry. *Archéologie du Nil Moyen* 9: 183-193.

Usai, D. 2014. Recent Advances in Understanding the Prehistory of Central Sudan. In Anderson and Welsby (eds.) 2014: 31-44.

Usai, D. 2016. A Picture of Prehistoric Sudan: The Mesolithic and Neolithic Periods. In *Oxford Handbooks Online*: 1-34. Oxford, Oxford University Press, (http://www.oxfordhandbooks.com/view/10.1093/oxfordhb/9780199935413.001.0001/oxfordhb-9780199935413-e-56).

Van Driel-Murray, C. 2000. Leatherworks and skin products. In Nicholson and Shaw (eds.) 2000: 299-319.

Valbelle, D. 2014. International Relations between Kerma and Egypt. In Anderson and Welsby (eds.) 2014: 103-109.

Vantini, G. 1975. *Oriental Sources Concerning Nubia*. Heidelberg and Warsaw, Akademie der Wissenschaften and Polish Academy of Sciences.

Vercoutter, J. 1994. L'Egypte et le désert de la Nubie entre Nil et Mer Rouge. *Sahara* 6: 63-68.

Vermeersch, P.M., Linseele, V., Marinova, E., Van Neer, W., Moeyersons, J. and Rethemeyer, J. 2015. Early and Middle Holocene Human Occupation of the Egyptian Eastern Desert: Sodmein Cave. *African Archaeological Review* 32: 465-503.

Welsby, D.A. 2002. *The Medieval Kingdoms of Nubia. Pagans, Christians and Muslims along the Middle Nile*. London, The British Museum Press.

Welsby, D.A. 2004. The Archaeology and History of Sudan. In D.A. Welsby and J.R. Anderson (eds.), *Sudan Ancient Treasures. An Exhibition of Recent Discoveries from the Sudan National Museum*: 12-17. London, The British Museum Press.

Welsby, D.A. (ed.) 2001. *Life on the desert edge: seven thousand years of settlement in the Northern Dongola Reach, Sudan*, Oxford, Archaeopress (*British Archaeological Reports* 980).

Wendorf, F. and Schild, R. 2002. Implications of Incipient Social Complexity in the Late Neolithic in the Egyptian Sahara. In R. Friedman (ed.) 2002: 13-20.

Wengrow, D. 2006. *The Archaeology of Early Egypt*. Cambridge, Cambridge University Press.

Weschenfelder, P. 2014. Linking the Eastern Desert and the Nile Valley: Pan-Grave People from the Late Middle Kingdom to the Early New Kingdom. In Anderson and Welsby (eds.) 2014: 357-366.

Whiteman, A.J. 1971. *The Geology of the Sudan Republic*. Oxford, Clarendon Press-Oxford University Press.

Wikens, G.E. 1982. Paleobotanical Speculations and Quaternary Environments in the Sudan. In M.A.J. Williams and D.A. Adamson (eds.), *A Land between Two Niles: Quaternary Geology and Biology of the Central Sudan*: 23-51. Rotterdam, Balkema.

Williams, M. A. J. 2009. Late Pleistocene and Holocene environments in the Nile basin. *Global and Planetary Change* 69: 1–15.

Williams, M.A.J., Usai, D., Salvatori, S., Williams, F.M., Zerboni, A., Maritan, L. and Linseele, V. 2015. Late Quaternary environments and prehistoric occupation in the lower White Nile valley, central Sudan. *Quaternary Science Reviews* 130: 72-88.

Williams, M. A. J., Williams, F. M., Duller, G. A. T., Munro, R. N., El Tom, O. A. M., Burrows, T. T., *et al.* 2010. Late Quaternary floods and droughts in the Nile valley, Sudan: New evidence from Optically Stimulated Luminescence and AMS radiocarbon dating. *Quaternary Science Reviews* 29: 1116–113.

Winchell, F. 2013. *The Butana Group Ceramics and their Place in the Neolithic and Post-Neolithic of Northeast Africa*. Oxford, Archaeopress (*Cambridge Monographs in African Archaeology* 83, British Archaeological Reports International Series 2459).

Worrall, G.A. 1960. Patchiness in Vegetation in the Northern Sudan. *Journal of Ecology* 48: 107-115.